Design against Crime
Beyond defensible space

Design against Crime

Beyond defensible space

Barry Poyner

Butterworths
London Boston Durban Singapore Sydney Toronto Wellington

First published 1983

© Barry Poyner 1983

British Library Cataloguing in Publication Data

Poyner, Barry
  Design against crime.
  1. Crime prevention   2. Crime and criminals
  3. Architecture, Domestic
  I. Title
  364.4'4   HV6177

  ISBN 0-408-01230-7

Library of Congress Cataloguing in Publication Data

Poyner, Barry
  Design against crime.
  Bibliography: p.
  Includes index.
  1. Crime prevention and architectural design.
  I. Title
  HV7431. P68 1983   364.4'9   83-7454

  ISBN 0-408-01230-7

Typeset by Butterworths Litho Preparation Department
Printed in Great Britain at the University Press, Cambridge

Foreword

by Sir Kenneth Newman, QPM
Commissioner, Metropolitan Police

From a Police viewpoint, Mr Poyner's book is useful and timely. It is useful because it lists in the form of readily assimilable 'patterns for design and management' ways in which the environment can be manipulated in order to reduce opportunities for committing crime. It is timely because the Police, faced with virtually static resources and ever increasing crime rates, are turning to crime prevention through environmental design as an approach that promises to be more effective than any traditional Police methods.

The book is useful and timely, too, because its publication coincides with the evolution of post-Scarman consultative committees in which local representatives, planners and other social agencies will join with Police with a view to addressing the substantive problems of crime control. Mr Poyner's material provides such committees not only with a handy reference to 'essential relationships within the environment which reduce the risk of one or more types of crime', but also with a clear illustration of the conceptual approach that will have to be adopted in such committees.

Police Crime Prevention Departments should also find the book a valuable addition to other works on situational prevention; a subject that is now being elevated to the mainstream of policing operations.

Finally, I would like to express my thanks to Mr Poyner for the assistance he has recently given the Metropolitan Police in analysis of environmental factors.

Acknowledgements

My thanks go to the Home Office for the research grant which enabled this book to be written. I would like to thank Dr Ron Clarke for originally suggesting this book, as well as acknowledging his considerable contribution to the development of the ideas behind situational crime prevention.

Tim Hope gave me much needed encouragement through the period of the project and, in a very practical way, helped me locate many of the references used in the work. Similarly, my wife Ann has helped in many ways, in both obtaining hard-to-come-by reference material and in checking through both draft manuscript and proofs.

The Tavistock Joint Library staff were very tolerant of the extra load this work has given them and I thank them for that. I would also like to thank Dr Richard Titus of the National Institute of Justice in Washington for providing so much valuable and up-to-date material. Frank Hartmann was kind enough to show me around Asylum Hill in Hartford, Connecticut. I have also not forgotten Sheena Wilson's generosity at passing on to me her collection of papers, which filled a number of important gaps.

Barry Poyner

Contents

1 Introduction

Are planners, architects and others who make decisions about how we manage our built environment partly responsible for the rise in crime?

There is no doubt that crime is rising in western developed countries and has been for many years. The increase is seen in official crime statistics, in surveys of potential victims and in opinion surveys on fear of crime. At the beginning of the 1960s Jane Jacobs launched an attack on city planning and design in her book *The Death and Life of Great American Cities*, drawing on her experience of living in New York and working as an architectural journalist. Among her targets was the abandoning of the traditional relationship of houses, sidewalks and street and its replacement with high-rise apartment blocks set in 'parks' along the lines of Le Corbusier's Radiant City thought up in the 1920s. She drew attention to the tendency for crime to occur in the large publicly accessible areas created by the newer forms of planning well away from conventional streets. Essentially, her criticism of new forms of design was that they broke down many of the traditional controls on criminal behaviour – the ability of residents to watch the street and the presence of people using the street both night and day.

A decade later Oscar Newman, an architect who, like Jane Jacobs worked in New York, published his now famous book *Defensible Space* (1972). Newman's target was similar to Jacob's but the intervening years had enabled him to research some of the problems of housing design and crime. Although it is true that Newman's research methods left a lot to be desired, his book convinced many that the form of modern buildings might have something to do with the increase in crime. He has certainly stimulated much research and many action projects aimed at reducing crime through the means of environmental change.

This book attempts to bring together the fruits of research that have followed in the wake of Newman's book, and which are concerned with the question of how far crime can be prevented by the design and management of the environment; findings come from the United States and England with some work from Canada. Researchers are also known to be active in France, Australia and New Zealand. The two principal sources of research funds have been the United States and United Kingdom Governments through what are now known as the National Institute of Justice in Washington and the Home Office Research and Planning Unit in London.

Although the original ideas of Jacobs and Newman need revision, there is little doubt that the design and management of urban environment does have a good deal to do with crime. As will be seen in various chapters of this book, the layout of neighbourhoods, the form of streets, the design of housing and the planning of schools can be said to contribute to the likelihood of crime. This can apply to the location of bus stops, the decision to use pay-as-you-enter buses, and even to the width of gangways between market stalls.

The task of preparing the book involved collecting all available published and unpublished work on research into crime prevention which involved some aspect of design and management

1

of the environment. The literature that was seen as possibly relevant to the project can be divided into several categories:
- Theoretical and descriptive writings on crime and the environment.
- Reports on empirical research or evaluations of action projects.
- Handbooks and similar published guidance on security design.

Theoretical and descriptive writings

A number of book reviews and other articles about Newman's theory of 'defensible space' have been produced by criminologists and designers. Many have been critical of both his formulation of theory in terms of territoriality (Hillier, 1973) and of his use of statistics (Bottoms, 1974). Pat Mayhew provides an excellent summary of these criticisms in her review of developments in defensible space theory (Mayhew, 1979). The general impression from these writings is a negative one, and they provide little that is of any direct value to the practitioner.

In parallel to the interest in Newman, another quite major area of study has continued to develop, which is a geographical approach to crime and the environment. Reviews of work in this area have been produced by Herbert (1977) and Davidson (1981) and there are a number of papers by the Brantinghams which are concerned with mapping techniques and will be of interest to planners (see, for example, Brantingham and Brantingham, 1981). The concern of these geographers is to explore, describe and attempt to explain the geographical distribution of crime. Together, these sources provide very absorbing insight into the geographical distribution of crime. However, from the point of view of the designer or manager there is not much guidance to be found from this kind of literature. To put it unfairly, it may be interesting to know that Florida has a higher murder rate than Ohio, but it is not a finding that brings us very near to knowing how to reduce the risk of murder

(except that a few rather nervous people might move house). It may be that the study of micro-distributions of crime will yield more prescriptive findings in time.

Empirical research and action projects

My preference in searching for material has been for research studies that produce good evidence that crime is less likely to occur under certain conditions. Buried under piles of books and papers about crime and crime prevention are relatively few which report findings from studies that had a good experimental design. Studies which explore environmental factors might compare two similar types of setting which differ in some specific way that is believed to reduce crime. Alternatively, they might be evaluations of locations before and after changes were made to try out some crime prevention idea. In some studies measures have been found to work, in others the evidence is uncertain or contrary to expectation. Of course, there are always problems of interpreting the results, but my aim has been to present the findings where there seems to have been a positive outcome from research.

Developing a book of this kind is a frustrating experience. So many of the reports on research studies, surveys or action project evaluations, particularly the several foot-high piles of reports from the United States, are written in a laborious and elaborately cautious style which makes reading hard work. Key facts in the understanding of the significance of a finding often remain buried obscurely in some corner of the report, and it may be only after several intensive searches that these facts are discovered.

The thinness of conclusions, which has been a characteristic of many of the projects, seems to correlate closely with the thickness of reports, as if the thinness of the results forces researchers to spend more time writing to justify their work to the funding body. It is all very understandable at that level, but it is quite dysfunctional to the dissemination of research findings. The increasing practice of producing 'executive summaries' is greatly appreciated, but even these can approach 40 000 words!

Handbooks and other guidance literature

There are a number of American publications which aim to set out guidance on how to go about planning for environmental crime prevention. Richard Gardiner (1978) for example produced a very attractive book on *Design for Safe Neighborhoods*. Although the book attempts to develop the ideas of Jane Jacobs and Oscar Newman, the main thrust of the work is to try to package them into a management consultancy approach to crime prevention. His subtitle of *The Environmental Security Planning and Design Process* is the more accurate. The Westinghouse team also emerged from a major programme of work under the title *Crime Prevention through Environmental Design* with an operational handbook (Wallis and Ford, 1980) which has similar qualities.

Admirable as I am sure these and similar books appear to the practitioner, they lack guidance about what solutions or measures actually work and in which situations. The solutions are left open ended: try this, try that, it all depends on the analysis. It is easy to say go make an analysis of the crime pattern, street traffic flows or pedestrian movement, but much more difficult to answer a crunch question like 'will stronger locks or improved lighting reduce burglary in this kind of neighbourhood'? If the 'experts' don't know the answer to this kind of question they should say so, and not weakly include 'use of stronger locks' and 'improve outdoor lighting' in a check list. I think that one reason for these handbooks to have emerged is to disguise the lack of knowledge and at least show some positive achievement from multi-million dollar programmes. Maybe they are also intended to act as a marketing aid for consultancy services!.

Apart from handbooks more directly concerned with environmental aspects of crime prevention, there is an extensive market of security handbooks of all kinds. These are aimed mainly at the security industry, particularly to industrial and commercial managements with major security problems. Many of these books suggest procedures for analysing the risk and other security problems, but their main content seems to be on the wide range of security systems and hardware now available as well as how to train and manage security personnel. Even though there is little doubt that some security systems are effective, it appears from this literature that there has been very little research or published evaluations of security systems. It is largely for this reason that little of this literature has been used as a source for this book. Consequently it has not been possible to include material on industrial and commercial security.

Types of crime

The types of crime that are open to prevention through design or management of the environment tend to be the more 'opportunist' types of crime. Crimes directed at the person include robbery, purse snatches and other thefts or larceny and some assaults – both violent and sexual assaults. Crimes against property include burglary (breaking and entering) and vandalism.

Although the studies often rely on victimisation data (surveys of potential victims) rather than police crime data, the definition of crime is based closely on what would normally be classified as a crime had it come to the notice of the police. One major area of uncertainty is the inclusion of research on vandalism. In the United States and Canada for example, vandalism is not recorded as a serious crime. In England and Wales there is a criminal offence of 'criminal damage' but there is a good deal of minor damage that would not come under this category.

Much vandalism in public housing and public places is regarded as a maintenance problem rather than a crime. Perhaps the most common form of vandalism is graffiti. As to whether this should be regarded as a crime, or even a delinquent act, is a moot point. Graffiti, for example, may be defacement of property, but it is also collected as a source of humour (see, for example, Rees, 1981). For all these reasons, research on vandalism is represented only by a few more important studies.

Patterns

Criminologists and other social scientists who work in this area are primarily concerned with scientific statements, rather than design statements. They express their findings in descriptive or predictive forms, or as hypotheses about the causes of crime. Designers express themselves in prescriptive forms, simply in terms of requirements and needs. The main task of this book has been to identify reasonably reliable scientific findings and express them in a prescriptive form. That is, attempt to define what is required if the scientific statement were true.

The means of presenting these prescriptions is in the form of *patterns* for design and management. The notion of *patterns* is based on the work of Christopher Alexander and his colleagues, who have been developing a 'pattern language' for building and planning. Their theory is that in designing or modifying the built environment, building or planning should be carried out according to well established patterns which connect or combine together in many differernt ways, much as we use language. Their book *A Pattern Language* was compiled as a source-book of patterns (Alexander *et al.*, 1977).

Figure 1.1 It is a moot point whether some vandalism should be regarded as crime. An example of graffiti on a bollard on the Hudson River front in New York. (Photo by author)

The *pattern* is probably the best means of communicating research findings to design and management professions. The pattern statements which are given throughout the following chapters attempt to define essential relationships within the environment which reduce the risk of one or more types of crime. The form of these statements is made as open and general as possible in order to give designers freedom to adapt them to situations which were not envisaged by those who did the original research. It is hoped that the patterns will not be seen as a set of restrictive requirements or recommendations. Mercifully, environmental crime prevention has not yet become the subject of government regulations, codes of practice and design standards as, for example, fire protection and safety. Although at least one British Chief Constable has advocated such mandatory control.

2 Crime prevention and the environment

Over the last decade an approach to crime prevention has emerged which may provide the most effective means of controlling the growth of crime in our society. This is sometimes referred to as the 'situational' approach to crime prevention (Clarke, 1980) and sometimes more specifically as 'crime prevention through environmental design'. It attempts to prevent crime by changing the situations in which crime occurs. For example, changes might be made to the design of products, buildings and public places, to the layout of streets and the planning of cities, and to the way facilities are managed, including some forms of policing and other supervision.

The environment has historically been designed to provide protection in times of social and political unrest. Mediaeval castles provided shelter for the surrounding inhabitants and walled towns of mediaeval Europe protected populations no larger than a neighbourhood of a modern American city. Even Baron Haussman's design for Paris in the mid-19th century provided a pattern of wide boulevards to facilitate the quick movement of mounted troops to put down riots or other civil unrest. But these more dramatic uses of the environment have given way to other forms of protection as society and its crime have changed.

In this century, the predominant approach to crime prevention by criminologists has aimed at changing the criminal rather than the crime situation. This approach assumed that criminals differ from the rest of society in some fundamental way which predisposes them to crime. Under this approach it is believed that if only the factors which cause this predisposition to crime can be properly identified, then means of crime prevention can be found. Factors which have been considered as causes of criminal behaviour include genetic or hereditary factors and factors associated with parental care, up-bringing and education.

In a collection of essays called *Thinking About Crime*, James Q. Wilson (1975) pointed out that, although such factors might be the 'root' causes of crime, there is not much that can be done through the social policies of governments to eliminate these causes. There is very little that governments can do to change attitudes to child-rearing or to inculcate habits of virtue and law-abidingness. 'If a child is delinquent because his family made him so or his friends encourage him to be so, it is hard to conceive what society might do about his attitudes. No one knows how a government might restore affection, stability and fair discipline to a family that rejects these characteristics'.

There have also been hopes of reducing crime through social policy in other more general ways. For example, because higher crime levels were often associated with slum neighbourhoods in the United States it was believed that a reduction in poverty through general rises in prosperity would reduce the level of crime. Wilson also drew attention to the inadequacy of such an explanation of crime in his essay *Crime Amidst Plenty: The Paradox of the Sixties* (Wilson, 1975). Crime soared in the United States in the early 1960s at a time when the country was experiencing a sustained period of prosperity. Some explanations for this seem obvious, like the increase in automobile thefts which followed the increased availability of cars (Gould, 1969);

but for the most part the increase in crime seems to have baffled the criminologists and policy makers alike. Wilson gives the impression that by the early 1970s there were many doubts in the minds of policy makers in the United States that crime could be effectively tackled through social policies.

Another area of policy aimed at reducing crime which had begun to raise doubts by the early 1970s was the sentencing and treatment of offenders. Rather than simply punish offenders it had long been believed that various forms of custodial and non-custodial sentences might reform the offender. Studies have been made of the effects of varying the length of sentence, the use of parole and probation as alternatives to prison. Comparisons have also been made of various custodial alternatives to prison such as Borstals, Detention Centres and Approved Schools. Some attempts have also been made to evaluate the effect of therapeutic regimes and other treatment programmes. Brody (1976) reviewed sixty-five of these studies for the Home Office. These were mainly from the UK and the United States, and he found that, in general, there was little difference in the effectiveness of different sentencing regimes, although some treatment programmes might have some value – for example, intensive counselling appeared effective for some types of offender.

Even if effective treatment regimes could be found to reform offenders, the value of this approach to crime prevention is limited because only a minority of offenders are caught. Less than half (40%) of serious crime reported to the police in England and Wales is 'cleared up' by the police (Home Office, 1981) and it is generally recognised that far more crime goes unreported. It is clear that many offenders will remain beyond the reach of any form of treatment.

This lack of success of both social policy and of criminal justice measures in reducing criminal behaviour has led to much greater interest in approaches to crime prevention which are directed more at the circumstances of the crime itself rather than the social and personality factors which give rise to it. For example, if we cannot effectively change the likely behaviour of the offender, is it possible to change the behaviour of the victims of crime, so that they are less likely to be victimised?

One of the most well established methods of crime prevention has been the use of publicity to persuade the public to take basic precautions to reduce crimes. There must be many thousands of leaflets produced by the police, public authorities, insurance companies and lock manufacturers giving advice about guarding their property, whether it is their home, car, or luggage, as well as advice on safe behaviour such as warning children to beware of strangers. Although there may be doubt about the value of some of this advice, there is little doubt that much crime could be prevented if the public took the precautions recommended. The problem, however, is that it is really quite difficult to persuade members of the public to act on advice given.

The problem has been admirably illustrated in a British study to find out whether press and poster campaigns and TV advertising do change the extent to which car drivers lock their cars when left parked in the street (Riley, 1980). Police checks on over 25 000 cars were made in three types of area, both before and after publicity campaigns. One area was subjected to a press and poster campaign, another to a TV advertisement campaign, and several other police areas were used for control observations. The findings showed that neither campaign had any effect on the behaviour of drivers.

Yet another well-established solution to crime prevention in the minds of public and policy-makers alike is the use of routine police patrolling. After an earlier tendency to withdraw from foot-patrolling to mobile patrol units much store has now been put by the use of increased patrolling and use of community-based police officers. Whilst it is clear that many benefits may come from community-based policing, including improved relations with the public, greater public reassurance and probably increased reportage of crime, there are reasons to doubt the extent to which such policing might prevent crime.

Some research has been done on the effectiveness of police patrols in the United States. As Kevin Heal (1982) points out in a recent summary of these issues, findings suggest that whilst it is probably true that police patrolling does have a deterrent effect on crime, any increase in resources over the present levels is unlikely to increase this effect. The only exceptions to this might be forms of street crime where specifically directed 'saturation' policing may have a useful effect over a limited area. The explanations given for this are that the geographical areas in which crime can occur are so great that the probability of a patrolling officer discovering a burglary or robbery is very small. Furthermore over half of the reported incidents occur in private places, beyond the reach of even the most efficient patrol.

Perhaps the realisation, however unconscious, that police patrolling is of limited value, prompted the development of citizen-based surveillance typically referred to as 'blockwatch'. The idea of using neighbourhood resources to reduce crime has become popular in the United States. Probably the best-researched example is the Community Crime Prevention Program at Seattle (Cirel *et al.*, 1977). Essentially this programme combined three elements: blockwatch, improved hardware security and property identification. Groups of neighbours were organised to watch each other's houses, some improvements were made to locks on doors and windows, and all valuables kept at home were marked with some form of personal identification.

There is little doubt from the two surveys carried out at Seattle that the Community Crime Prevention Program did have a beneficial effect. There were fewer burglaries to the houses included in the Program, whereas those not included continued to suffer similar rates as before. There was also apparently no displacement of crime from areas included in the Program to other areas. However, the effect of the Program appeared to last for little more than twelve months. This fact in itself suggests that the permanent changes included in the Program (marking valuables and improving locks) had contributed little to the success of the Program. Indeed, Irvin Waller (1979) has argued that the idea of simply adding a stronger lock to a front door, inserting nails in window frames or placing wooden rods in sliding door guides, is little more than a 'security illusion' (see also Chapter 4). Identifying valuable property with the owner's driving licence number or social security number, he also considers of little value.

The assumption of identification of valuables is that this will make it more difficult to 'fence' stolen goods. The effectiveness of this is doubted because it is now believed that most stolen goods are sold direct rather than to the public. In any case the effectiveness of marking would only be significant if extensive routine checks were made by the police. Also the ease with which numbers could be removed or disguised all adds to doubt about the effectiveness of this method.

The reason for the short-lived success of the Seattle programme, according to Waller, was that the blockwatch system involved neighbours in a number of co-operative activities such as mowing lawns and clearing snow when houses were unoccupied for a time, which gave the impression that houses were occupied. For this, Waller coined the term 'occupancy proxy'. Similarly there may have been some deterrent from the posting of a decal or sticker warning that all the valuable goods on the premises have been marked. But it is quite easy to imagine how such effects can be short-lived.

In summary, community-based crime prevention programmes involving blockwatch and other neighbourly efforts to disguise absences from property do seem to work as a crime prevention method. However, they are short-lived and require 'recharging' at regular intervals. It is impossible to know how easily this can be done. It certainly would require determined organisation at local level. Nevertheless these programmes may be appropriate where no other form of crime prevention can be found.

Defensible space
With this rather discouraging failure of so many approaches to the prevention of crime, it was not surprising that so much interest was shown in the ideas of Oscar Newman, when his book *Defensible Space* was first published in 1972. His theory was essentially an approach to solving the problem of designing multi-unit public housing projects in urban America. Newman like Jacobs was concerned that 'The public areas of a multi-family residential environment . . . can make the act of going from street to apartment equivalent to running the gauntlet.' He believed that it was possible to design housing projects in such a way that the residents would be able to gain control over spaces immediately adjacent to their homes and deter strangers and potential criminals.

His theory proposed four elements of physical design which act individually or in combination to contribute to the creation of secure environments:

1 *Territoriality* – The sub-division and zoning of communal space in and around residential buildings to promote proprietary attitudes among residents.
2 *Natural surveillance* – The positioning of apartment windows to allow residents to naturally survey the exterior and interior public areas of their living environment.
3 *Image* – The use of building forms and idioms to avoid the stigma of public housing (which Newman sees as a specifically American problem).
4 *Milieu* – Locating residential projects to face onto areas of the city considered safe (such as heavily-trafficked streets, institutional areas and government offices).

Newman's work was very much in the spirit of his time. It reflects the growing interest of the architectural profession in the relation between environment and behaviour, with some influence from rather popularised anthropology and ideas of territoriality drawn from writings on ethology by authors such as Robert Ardrey (1966). He was also deeply conscious of the poor condition of much high-rise public housing and his photographs of heavily vandalised lobbies and access areas and rather forlorn open spaces between bleak and forbidding apartment blocks (*Figures 2.1* and *2.2*) could not fail to trigger sympathetic responses from architects, planners, housing managers or indeed anyone concerned with the social problems of our modern world.

Because his emphasis was on the use of the environment to promote resident control and therefore somehow return to a more human and less threatening environment, 'defensible space' seemed to offer a much more attractive alternative to the hardline security measures already being introduced to housing. Hitherto the only solution to crime and vandalism on public housing estates was the use of target hardening and physical security measures. Efforts were concentrated on increasing the robustness and damage resistance of materials and components such as doors and lifts. Access was reduced by fencing off damaged areas, locking doors, using electronic surveillance systems in lifts and lobbies, and using entry intercoms. Housing projects were beginning to look like fortresses rather than the attractive living environments envisaged by the designers.

In the United States it was not just in housing that the problem was getting serious. Schools also presented a serious problem (see Chapter 7). The continuing increase of vandalism, burglary and other crime in American schools had led to the frequent use of security patrols with the use of dogs and an increased use of electronic surveillance systems.

The fear of fortress-like housing, schools and other facilities is understandable, because one of the characteristics of 'adding on' security mea-

Figure 2.1 An example from Newman's book *Defensible Space* of a heavily vandalised lift lobby on a housing project in Philadelphia. (Newman, 1972:104) (Courtesy Oscar Newman)

Figure 2.2 An illustration of interior grounds of a public housing project in Brooklyn, New York. Residents viewed these areas as the most dangerous in the project. (Newman, 1973:54) (Courtesy Oscar Newman)

sures to existing situations is the risk of having to go on escalating the measures. Protective fencing is often broken down and has to be replaced by stronger fencing, perhaps topped by barbed wire. Chains and locks may be broken and have to be replaced by stronger locks and chains. William Brill (1973) cites an American example of how youths managed to overcome an elaborate surveillance system which controlled access to an apartment building. They first broke the system and then carefully watched the repairman at work. They were able to gain access to the top of the lift, stop the lift, open the hatch on top and demand that the passengers hand up their valuables and sometimes clothing. All the guard in the basement could do was watch on the TV monitor the bizarre spectacle of people passing their wallets and clothes upwards, out of the range of the TV camera.

The attractiveness of Newman's ideas was that, although he did not rule out the use of fences or even electronic surveillance, his main aim was to find ways of changing the underlying structure of the environment so that it would not attract criminal behaviour, and that it would enable residents to control access to their homes and the use of surrounding areas. It has been very much in this spirit that further work has developed. It has been an attempt to find ways of improving the inherent security of design and planning forms without relying on 'added on' security measures.

Crime prevention through environmental design (CPTED)

Newman's ideas had a major impact on the programme of research supported by the United States Government through the then National Institute of Law Enforcement and Criminal Justice. A number of demonstration projects were launched to explore the idea of preventing crime through environmental design and improvement. The main body through which this work was done was the Westinghouse National Issues Center. Whereas Newman's work was evolved from the problems of housing design, these demonstration projects attempted to explore crime prevention in a variety of different settings: commercial, residential neighbourhoods and schools. The projects involved a commercial strip at Portland, Oregon, residential neighbourhoods at Minneapolis and Hartford, Connecticut, and four high schools in Broward County, Florida.

Those working on the projects attempted to broaden the strategies which would be used in design from that used by Newman. Generally, they were grouped under four headings: surveillance, movement control, activity support, and motivational reinforcement. It may be worth summarising the range of tactics covered by these headings and referred to in *Crime Prevention Through Environmental Design: An Operational Handbook* (Wallis and Ford, 1980).
1 *Surveillance* – The purpose of surveillance is to increase the risk of a potential offender being observed, and therefore identified and apprehended. Suggested tactics included improved lighting, the removal of blind spots in movement areas, the use of windows or electronic surveillance devices, locating vulnerable areas near busy places and introducing supervisory personnel, police or security guards or a blockwatch.
2 *Movement control* – Any measures that can limit the movement of a potential offender through a site. It included both Newman's ideas of real and symbolic barriers associated with the idea of territoriality, and also all the security hardware of locks. Specific tactics included reducing the number of entrances, allowing keyed access to zones within a building, street closure, controlled access to neighbourhoods, and management of facilities to reduce congestion.
3 *Activity support* – Increasing human use of areas by making them more attractive or by rearranging facilities: this in turn enhances surveillance. Methods include creating activity areas, providing information kiosks, display

areas, portable theatres for street activity, clustering commercial establishments with similar operating hours, and diversifying land use.

4 *Motivational reinforcement* – This is necessary alongside the physical changes to enhance the desire of people to engage in crime prevention activity. The tactics suggested were less well defined but include the encouragement of personalised environments, better maintained public areas, co-operation between business men, community development programmes, improved police/community relations, and the involvement of citizens in setting police priorities.

The rich diversity of ideas that has gone into these demonstration projects has been their downfall from the research point of view. Undoubtedly, many of these tactics can contribute to a reduction in crime in the appropriate setting, but when they are all bundled together in the same demonstration project it is almost impossible to decide those tactics which are the most effective and those which should be applied elsewhere. If the demonstrations had been an enormous success then all caution might have been thrown to the wind and the whole package of measures accepted as a highly desirable range of solutions to crime prevention. Sadly, this was not the case. Although some encouraging signs can be found in the results, all four projects have presented major problems of interpretation, and very few clear findings have emerged (see also Chapters 3 and 7).

A good illustration of these research problems can be found in the use of street lighting as a crime-prevention measure. James Tien and his colleagues were commissioned to review the street lighting projects funded by the United States Federal Government as a means of crime prevention (Tien *et al.*, 1979). In most cases the original plan for the projects had been to include a proper evaluation of the effect of the improved lighting on crime rates. However, the government funding sources expected quick results, and so evaluations had to be completed within eighteen months of funding. Delays in the early stages reduced the period available for evaluation, and since delays are more the rule than the exception, project evaluations were nearly always done over a shorter period than planned.

Some evaluations were based on only one or two months' of crime statistics, where originally twelve months' data had been considered minimal. Budget overruns also curtailed evaluation efforts, which in some cases had been cancelled. From over a hundred crime-related street lighting projects, only fifteen had some formal evaluation that was available to the review team.

Not surprisingly, the review team were very critical of the evaluations which were carried out. The research designs were considered inadequate, statistical analyses were often inappropriate and the findings produced were rarely statistically significant. The team concluded that there were no clear indications that crime was actually prevented by improved street lighting; indeed some evaluations even showed that crime increased after the installation of new lighting. The only conclusion which they felt was justified was that street lighting did reduce residents' fear of crime. Even so, when it is realised what kind of question was asked of residents in these evaluation surveys, it is difficult to believe that the surveys accurately measured changes in the feelings of residents. The report quotes a typical question as 'Since the addition of the new street lights, do you feel safer, the same or not as safe?'. On such an emotive subject area for the United States, this is a very leading question and unlikely to produce reliable answers.

Situational crime prevention research in England
At the same time as the demonstration projects were being mounted in the United States, a number of rather more carefully designed research studies were initiated by the Home Office Research Unit in London. The earlier studies have been gathered together by Clarke and

Mayhew (1980) in a book *Designing Out Crime*, but further studies have now been completed which have more specific implications for design of the environment and which appear in Chapters 4, 6 and 7.

The approach taken by the Home Office Research Unit (now the Research and Planning Unit) has been broadly based on a wide range of situational factors, which have included publicity campaigns to try to change victim behaviour and some forms of patrolling. But it is clear that the most positive results have emerged from studies of factors related to environmental design and management. The introduction to *Designing Out Crime* summarised the situational measures which the editors believe to be effective as follows:

1 *Target hardening* – The most obvious approach to security which included the use of stronger locks and other security hardware. In the case of vandalism, the use of stronger and more robust materials which would resist damage.

2 *Target removal* – The most common form of this is where cash is substituted by other forms of payment to reduce the risk of theft or robbery as, for example, where the risk of a wages snatch would disappear when employees were paid by cheque.

3 *Removing the means to crime* – Examples given by the editors included gun control and, in the case of pubs which suffer from violence, the use of plastic containers for drinks rather than glasses.

4 *Reducing the pay-off* – An uncertain category which included the marking of valuable property in the hope that this would discourage theft.

5 *Formal surveillance* – The use of police or security personnel to patrol or guard. The authors also mention blockwatch.

6 *Natural surveillance* – The form of surveillance referred to by Oscar Newman whereby residents or users of an environment can, during their normal patterns of activity, keep watch on any potential crime target.

7 *Surveillance by employees* – This lies between 5 and 6 above and includes the use of people such as doormen in apartment buildings, caretakers on housing estates, shop assistants and car park attendants. The staff employed on public transport probably play a major role in preventing potential crime.

8 *Environmental management* – One successful example of this is the management of football supporters. Rival supporters are carefully segregated and escorted to prevent fighting. Transport is carefully scheduled to take visiting supporters away from the area as soon as possible after the match to reduce violence and vandalism. Another example, referred to in Chapter 5, is the control of child density to reduce vandalism on housing estates through housing allocation policies.

Present knowledge
It would be foolish to pretend that this new subject area has already developed to maturity. It would be equally foolish for the practising designer or anyone else concerned with the design and management of the environment to expect that a complete set of precise guidelines can now be set down for environmental crime prevention. However, there is now sufficient research material available for a good start to be made in setting down and organising this knowledge in a form that can be used by administrators, managers, practitioners and researchers; hence, this book.

The following chapters of this book cover the main topics of research into environmental crime prevention that have begun to generate useful findings. Chapter 3 presents some of the work on urban neighbourhoods which is a common topic in the American research. Chapter 4 deals with residential burglary which is the topic area that has received the greatest research effort. Chapters 5, 6 and 7 present smaller bodies of research on vandalism on housing estates, street attacks in city centres and mainly burglary in schools. Chapter 8 brings together findings from a number of research studies on public transport.

From the findings presented, it is possible to generalise about the ways in which the environment can reduce crime. Perhaps the first thing to notice is that Newman's ideas about territoriality have never been validated by research, even though a number of researchers have tried. However, the concept which seems to have relaced territoriality is *accessibility*. Curiously, although 'access control' featured among the measures for CPTED it was not included in the Home Office categories. Chapters 3 and 4 of this book will show that limiting access to neighbourhoods and residential streets can reduce crime. Also, at a more specific level, the limiting of access to the communal areas of apartment buildings and to the backs of houses can reduce burglary.

Natural surveillance was part of Newman's defensible space theory which has survived the rigours and vagaries of all the research programmes on the topic. It is the only category to be included in both the CPTED and the Home Office categories. Natural surveillance has been found to be important in the control of residential burglary and in the reduction of break-ins to schools. It is also relevant to the control of vandalism in multi-unit housing. *Formal surveillance* might be cost-effective where there are specific concentrations of crime such as in city centre retail markets. *Surveillance by employees* is particularly relevant to public transport facilities, and it is referred to in connection with school caretakers.

Target hardening and removal are certain to be valuable forms of environmental crime prevention, but they have been relatively neglected

Figure 2.3 Suburban housing in the United States often has no barrier to access around the house to the back yard. This example is from a middle-class neighbourhood near Washington D.C. (Photo by author)

by researchers. Some research on target hardening against residential burglary is discussed in Chapter 4 which reveals that the issue is not as simple as most crime prevention literature would have us believe.

Environmental management is also represented in the book in that housing allocation policies that control child densities on estates have been shown to influence the levels of vandalism. There is also a general belief that quick repair and effective maintenance policies reduce property damage. One finding in Chapter 7 suggests that well kept school buildings and grounds discourage crime.

The general conclusion from the findings presented in this book is that the form of the urban environment can and does create opportunities for crime. For example, the use of large multi-unit design forms for public housing projects created more opportunities for crime than would have happened if all public housing had been built as single-family houses or row houses. Similarly, modern school designs which sprawl across a large campus can also be claimed to create more opportunities for crime than earlier forms of school design (see Chapter 7).

It is interesting to speculate on some of the differences between design forms in the United States and Europe. Have some of these differences contributed to the higher crime rates in the United States? If, as seems virtually certain from research, street patterns that give easy through access to residential areas facilitate crime opportunities, then have the block and grid patterns that are so common in North American cities made crime easier to commit there than in the less regular street patterns of Britain and other parts of Europe which provide less through access?

Similarly, it is interesting to note how different the accessibility and surveillance characteristics are between suburban housing in the United States and Britain. The findings in Chapter 4 on residential burglary show that quite different risks exist for detached and terraced (or row)

Figure 2.4 Modern suburban housing in England has open fronts but high walls or fences to prevent access to back gardens. This example is in Hertfordshire. (Photo by author)

houses, and that high walls or fences around back yards or gardens reduce burglary risk. Typically, modern suburban houses in the United States are detached and often have unfenced access all round the house whereas in Britain terraced and semi-detached houses are more common with back gardens fenced with locked or bolted side access. Elsewhere in Europe even greater protection is given to houses. For example in the South of France both large and small houses have locked access gates at the front of the plot with delivery services not normally allowed beyond the gate. So far these cultural differences in design have not been researched, but it does seem possible that they could explain at least some of the differences in crime patterns for different countries.

Figure 2.5 Even quite modest villas in the south of France have high walls or wire-mesh fences around the perimeter of the plot. The gates are full height and usually kept locked. Deliveries and post etc. are left at the gate, which is now commonly fitted with an intercom system. (Photo by author)

14

3 Safer neighbourhoods

One of the strongest characteristics of the American research literature on crime prevention and the environment is the focus on *neighbourhoods*. The reasons for this are partly emotive and also emerge from the belief that crime prevention is something that can be achieved through the community. Newman's ideas about defensible space, territoriality and the notion of informal social control lead inevitably to the belief that crime levels might be reduced by some combination of design measures and community action or development. This is certainly the case for Richard Gardiner in his *Design of Safe Neighborhoods*:

'*In dealing with the relationship between opportunity crimes and the physical environment, the neighborhood is the natural geographic and social unit to work with. First and foremost, it is the neighborhood that acts as the interface between home and city and provides opportunity for human interaction and cooperation. The neighborhood is the scale at which communal standards of behavior are first formed . . . If crime cannot be controlled at the neighborhood, it will eventually undermine the entire city*'. *(Gardiner, 1978:5).*

It is believed that if people feel they can rely on the co-operation and support of other residents, they may feel more confident about intervening to prevent a criminal act. Also, if they know their near neighbours, they will be better able to identify strangers, and again act either by intervening themselves or at least by reporting suspicious behaviour to the police. The corollary of this is that if it is known, or somehow recognised, that this pattern of behaviour is present in a neighbourhood, it would act as a deterrent to would-be criminals.

Closing streets

A clear illustration of this kind of thinking is presented by Oscar Newman in his study of *The Private Streets of St Louis*, from a study originally reported in 1974 but published formally in his second book, *Community of Interest* (Newman, 1975, 1980). Here the turn-of-the-century developments for wealthy communities, built on the periphery of the then expanding city of St Louis, had been built as private streets – the residents owning the streets and being responsible for their maintenance.

As social and economic change proceeded, these streets became deprivatised but, by the 1950s, the middle-class residents began to form new private-street associations. These associations reacquired the ownership of the streets from the city (a precedent already existed for private streets in the city by-laws). When these streets were privatised, in addition to changing the legal ownership of the street or groups of streets, the physical nature of the street was also changed. One end is blocked to make it a cul-de-sac, avoiding any through traffic, and the other end is usually defined positively by a narrowing of the entrance to the street and sometimes with a portal or similar symbolic treatment of the entrance (see *Figures 3.1* and *3.2*).

The residents of these private streets claim that the physical closure of the streets and their legal association act together to create social

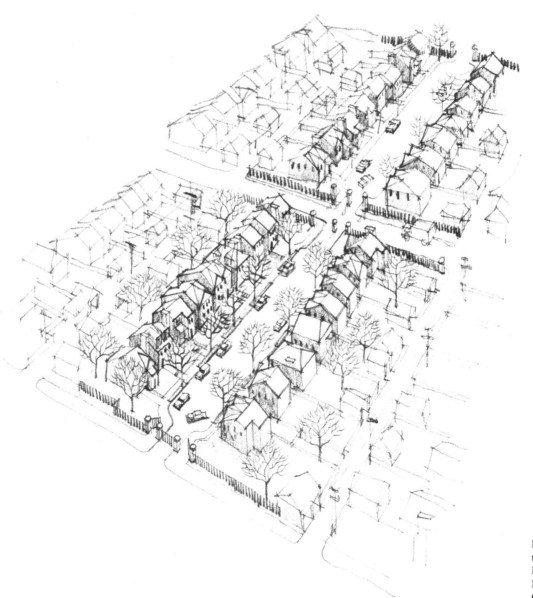

Figure 3.1 Aerial view of a typical private street in St Louis, Missouri (from Newman, 1980). (Courtesy Oscar Newman)

cohesion, stability and security. The deed restrictions mean that residents pay the cost of maintenance of the streets (although there is a small tax abatement). The restrictions also force owners to retain single-family residential occupation which, as will be seen later, seems to be an important factor in crime reduction.

One of the interesting features of the streets described by Newman is that they have not gone through a gentrification process, as have so many other areas that have reduced crime problems. These streets have simply maintained their middle-class occupancy and single-family occupancy over the years, while neighbouring streets have undergone drastic social and economic changes. The private streets attracted young families who like to live in a more urban setting and liked the quality of the older house property. They were prepared to move in because they were confident that property values in these private streets would be maintained and probably increase. The process develops a homogeneous neighbourhood, a group of residents with shared values about home ownership – association of like-minded, economically similar and committed residents. Newman calls this a 'community of interest':

'There is little pedestrian and vehicular traffic through the private streets and their physical separation provides one with the distinct feeling that the closed streets can resist the change taking place around them'. (Newman 1980:131)

The idea of residents having a sense of control is also essential to the success of the private streets. Newman quotes from his research interviews:

'. . . Closing the street gives the area a different feeling. If it is closed, you have the feeling of control and that you are living on your own turf.'

The research did attempt to measure the differences in crime rates between private and non-privatised streets, and the study showed that the non-privatised streets had more street crime (burglaries were not differentiated). Newman had previously been criticised in his presentation of defensible space ideas for underplaying the social and economic variables, and here again there was a difficulty. The private streets had become socially and economically different from the non-private streets. Although both private and public streets had black and white residents, property in private streets was owned and occupied by single middle-income families. The non-

Figure 3.2 Example of symbolic gateway to private street from Newman, 1980). (Courtesy Oscar Newman)

privatised streets had similar properties which had been sub-divided into multi-family rented units, some of which had become so deteriorated that they had been demolished. The residents were mainly low-income groups. It is easy to say that the reason for private streets to have less crime is that they do not suffer the same social problems of urban decline, but Newman would argue, quite reasonably, that it was privatisation which prevented the social decline of these streets.

Newman and his colleagues also collected some information on residents' feelings about safety. Residents in the private streets felt that their streets were safer than the neighbourhood as a whole, while those in neighbourhood public streets felt that their streets were unsafe. The researchers also made observations of the streets to record the behaviour in the two kinds of street. They found that residents in private streets were much more likely to leave windows open facing the street, more likely to leave possessions unguarded on their lawns, porches or sidewalks. Car doors or windows were also more likely to be left open in the private streets.

There is little doubt that the private streets of St Louis do have less crime and the residents feel safer. But how far can these ideas be applied elsewhere? There were several special factors operating in these streets which may not be present elsewhere. The area had a special character, it was near a university and its medical facilities; there was a large park which provided recreational resources – a zoo, golf courses, lakes, playing fields, etc.

The ideas embodied in the private streets are an extension of Newman's interest in what he has called 'territoriality'. This seems to mean that people will feel more able to extend their control over their immediate surroundings and in some way this has been believed to reduce crime because it might discourage potential offenders, who would be more likely to be challenged or observed doing crime. Residents with a greater commitment to their area may more likely call the police or intervene themselves if they see something suspicious.

In addition to this psychological idea of 'territoriality' there is the more practical idea of restricting access. By blocking off streets, there is less excuse for potential offenders to be wandering or driving about looking for targets to burgle or rob. Closure of streets will reduce the usage to those who live, legitimately visit or serve residents. The lack of through traffic might also change the character in terms of noise and patterns of use so that again there is less cause for strangers to be in the street and those who use the street become known, or will be recognised as strangers.

These ideas are a fusion of social and environmental design ideas, and it is not surprising to find they are ideas which appeal to planners, designers and those interested in the social well being of communities. The ideas have been applied in other places in the United States, not always primarily for crime prevention reasons. Some examples are given as case studies in Gardiner's book *Design for Safe Neighborhoods* (Gardiner, 1978).

The most interesting of these projects, and certainly the one which has had the most thorough evaluation, is at Asylum Hill in Hartford, Connecticut. Asylum Hill is a residential area near the business and insurance centres of Hartford. In the early part of the 1970s this attractive area, consisting primarily of low-rise buildings used as two- or three-family dwellings, was becoming an undesirable neighbourhood. Landlords were reluctant to maintain the housing stock. Long-term residents were leaving. Major factors in this incipient decline were thought to be rising rates of robbery and burglary and the fear they engendered.

The population was transient and about equal black and white. Because the majority of the housing stock was small units in old houses, the population was mainly single people renting. Families with children were in a distinct minority. Such a population is clearly different from the private streets of St Louis, but they were not poor, having an income about average for the city.

The result of the assessment made by a team of consultants was a programme aimed at three parallel lines of action. It included proposals for changing the physical environment, for changes in the organisation of policing and the encouragement of community groups and residents' organisations. One of the problems was seen to be the extent to which the streets of the area were used by through traffic. In order to begin a process of trying to encourage residents to take more interest in their neighbourhood, physical changes were made to the streets. Some access to side streets was narrowed to discourage use and to symbolise some degree of 'territoriality' or at least symbolise privatisation. Some streets were closed to make cul-de-sacs.

The scheme is shown in *Figure 3.3*. The entrances to neighbourhood streets were narrowed and defined symbolically by large planters as shown in *Figure 3.4*. One or two streets were made one way. At the same time the police agreed to create a neighbourhood police team. The purpose of this was to try to build a closer relationship between the police and the residents by having the same group of police officers working permanently only in the one area. This would enable their local knowledge to be more detailed and to build up a committee of police and residents to improve communication and create a means whereby residents might influence priorities for police activity.

On reflection the street changes were modest. Indeed there was considerable difficulty gaining agreement with all the many interests involved, not least the re-routing of buses, which was never achieved, and the problem of providing for emergency vehicles (see *Figure 3.5*). In particular, nothing was achieved in reducing pedestrian access across the neighbourhood, particularly the movement of children to and from school. Although the police team was retained for the period immediately after the project was set up, by the time a second evaluation was made in 1979, the police team had been disbanded.

In the first evaluation of this project (Fowler *et al.*, 1979 and Hollander *et al.*, 1980) there appears to be clear evidence that the project is working to some extent. They relied on survey data drawn from residents in Asylum Hill and from elsewhere in the city for control purposes. Police data were not used for the purposes of

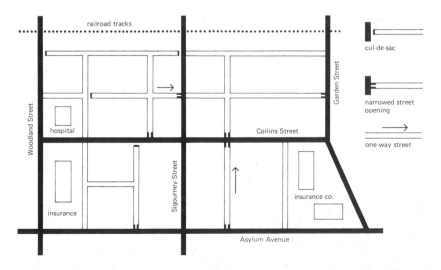

Figure 3.3 Street changes in North Asylum Hill (from Hollander *et al.*, 1980:30)

Figure 3.4 An access point from a through road to a non-through road at Asylum Hill. The roadway is narrowed with planters placed to define a symbolic gateway. (Photo by author)

monitoring the effect on crime of the changes made by the project, although they were used to plot distributions of crimes on maps and to locate the addresses of those offenders who had been arrested. The study relied mainly on victimisation data from residents. Essentially, they found that both burglary and robbery (including purse snatches) had been reduced in the year after the physical changes were completed. The numbers were small, and so there was some

statistical uncertainty as to whether there had been a real reduction in robbery and purse snatches.

Perhaps one of the most interesting changes in the pattern of crime was that, when the police-reported crimes were plotted, there was a significant shift from side-street to main-street locations for crimes, particularly robbery and purse snatches (*Figures 3.6* and *3.7*). Before programme completion, the side streets had 64% of the

Figure 3.5 A blocked end of a cul-de-sac at Asylum Hill. The roadway is paved over with a raised concrete area on which planters are positioned but with space to allow emergency vehicles access. No doubt some drivers will use this access illicitly. (Photo by author)

robberies, but the year after only 42%. The change of distribution seemed to be brought about by the physical changes to the streets (see *Table 3.1*).

When a second evaluation was undertaken in 1979, two years after the first, the findings were disappointing (Fowler and Mangione, 1982). It was found, using the same source of survey data on victimisation, that the crime levels were back to what might have been expected had nothing been done to the area. However, some reassurance could be gained by the fact that 'social organisation and informal social control' had continued to grow. Residents used the neighbourhood more, they walked in it more, they had more arrangements with neighbours to watch each other's houses, they found it easier to recognise strangers and claimed to have intervened more often in a 'suspicious neighbourhood situation'. Fear of crime had not reduced but it was found not to have increased to the same extent as elsewhere in the city.

It would be foolish to dismiss such findings as confusing or just useless. They were well researched over a period from 1973 to 1979, and it is unlikely that many similar sets of data will be produced elsewhere. One important fact is that the introduction of the street changes did make a significant difference in crime for a while. This cannot be said of the other two elements in the programme: the social programme and the neighbourhood police team. The consultations with residents began as early as 1974 and involved questions of implementing the street changes and the police liaison committee. Social improvements came gradually throughout the period of study and it would seem difficult to say from this data available that these had any real effect on crime. What might be reasonably claimed is that better social organisation and informal control may have influenced the levels of fear or concern about crime which, although not improved, did not increase as elsewhere in the city. It could be said that the return to a higher crime rate can be blamed on the problems

TABLE 3.1 Location of street robberies in Asylum Hill *(from Hollander et al., 1980:30)*

	Before programme completion 1976	After programme completion 1977
Target Area (North Asylum Hill)		
Main street	36%	58%
Side street	64%	42%
Total %	100	100
Control Area (South Asylum Hill)		
Main street	42%	52%
Side street	58%	48%
Total %	100	100

associated with the police team. Pressures on manpower and other problems for the Hartford police led to the withdrawal of the team and indeed a generally lower level of police activity. But this explanation is insufficient because data were recorded in the surveys for both North and South Asylum Hill. South Asylum Hill was included in the area where the neighbourhood police team operated but excluded from the street changes, which only occurred in North Asylum Hill. The crime levels remained stable through the period of study in South Asylum Hill, suggesting that the team policing by itself had very little effect on crime.

The fact that crime did reduce immediately following the introduction of street changes seems to indicate that there was some causal link. Clearly the physical changes would be seen by everyone using the area and they may have had at least some short-term effect on behaviour. Certainly there were reductions in both traffic and pedestrian counts in 1977. The combination of the symbolic barriers and the reduction of access may well help to explain the reduction in crime. However, the evidence from the 1979

ASYLUM HILL DISTRICT

STREET ROBBERIES
JULY 1975 – JUNE 1976

● MAIN STREET ROBBERY · 72
■ SECONDARY STREET ROBBER'

HARTFORD ANTI·CRIME PROJECT
Hartford Connecticut

UNITED STATES DEPARTMENT OF JUSTICE
LAW ENFORCEMENT ASSISTANCE ADMINISTRATION

CONTRACTOR:
The Hartford Institute of Criminal and Social Justice
SUBCONTRACTORS:
Richard A. Gardner & Associates · Planning and Design
Survey Research Program U-Mass Boston &
The Joint Center for Urban Studies of M.I.T. and Harvard
Urban Systems Research & Engineering Inc.

National Institute Grant No. 73-NI-99-0044-G

0 100 200   400   600   800
SCALE

Figure 3.6 Location of
street robberies in Asylum
Hill before street changes
(from Gardiner, 1978)

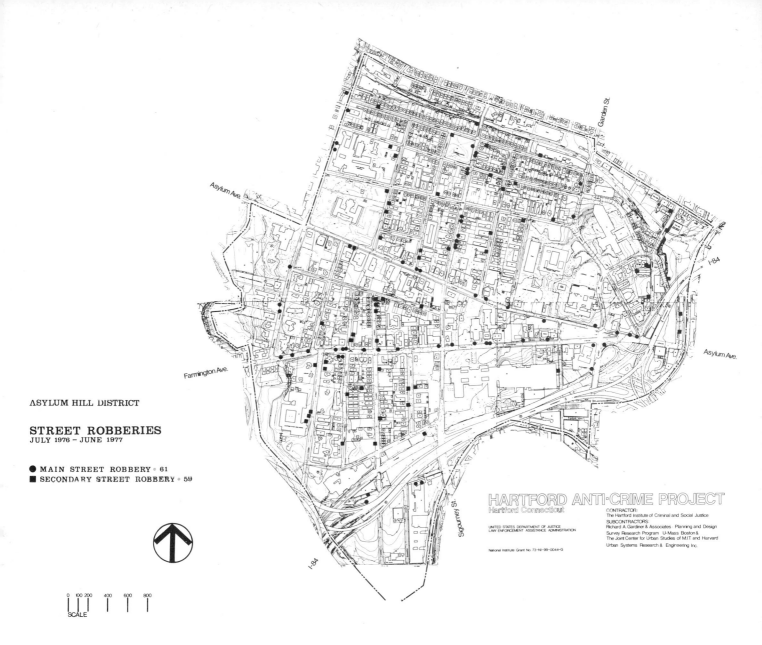

ASYLUM HILL DISTRICT

STREET ROBBERIES
JULY 1976 – JUNE 1977

● MAIN STREET ROBBERY · 61
■ SECONDARY STREET ROBBERY · 59

Asylum Ave.

Garden St.

I-84

Asylum Ave.

Farmington Ave.

Sumner St.

I-84

HARTFORD ANTI-CRIME PROJECT
Hartford Connecticut

CONTRACTOR:
The Hartford Institute of Criminal and Social Justice
SUBCONTRACTORS:
Richard A. Gardiner & Associates · Planning and Design
Survey Research Program · U-Mass Boston &
The Joint Center for Urban Studies of M.I.T. and Harvard
Urban Systems Research & Engineering Inc.

UNITED STATES DEPARTMENT OF JUSTICE
LAW ENFORCEMENT ASSISTANCE ADMINISTRATION

National Institute Grant No. 73-NI-99-0044-G

0 100 200   400   600   800
SCALE

Figure 3.7 Location of
street robberies in Asylum
Hill after street changes
(from Gardiner, 1978)

23

survey is quite interesting in showing how this impact on behaviour changed. Although traffic counts continued to go down, pedestrian counts had greatly increased to well above the original pre-programme average. Indeed this was reinforced through observations by both survey teams and the police that there were more groups of teenagers and men loitering in the park and streets, and also the problem of drunken men had increased. Crime had also moved back into the side streets in 1979.

It has already been mentioned that there was little done to reduce the access of pedestrians into the area. The measures taken to reduce vehicular access and symbolise less access, whilst adequate to reduce traffic permanently, could not have a permanent effect on pedestrian use. The now quieter streets of North Asylum Hill became regarded as more pleasant; indeed, property values had begun to rise as a result of the reduction in traffic. When this was coupled with a decline in police activity, potential criminals were attracted onto the streets, perhaps interested in burglary of the now more valued residential accommodation.

Two questions seem important but must remain unanswered from this project:
1 Would far more dramatic physical changes to access, particularly for pedestrians, have reduced the use of the streets by non-resident loitering groups?
2 Would the continued deployment of a neighbourhood police team have been sufficient to control these matters, by simply moving groups on and dealing with drunks etc?

The evidence, for what it is, would suggest positive answers to both questions. There seems little doubt, looking at *Figures 3.3–3.5*, that the physical changes are very modest. It is also easily appreciated that the discouragement of loitering, etc. is a common element in normal police work.

The conclusion which should perhaps be drawn from these projects is that closure of streets to through traffic and pedestrian movement must be fairly rigorous, such as only one pedestrian/car access to a cul-de-sac, and making it appear relatively private with some constriction or gateway, etc to symbolise the restricted access. This should then be reinforced by some specific socio-legal change (such as common legal rights and responsibilities) or by security patrolling to police the access idea and to make sure that people behave as the physical design implies.

The pattern which is suggested from these two examples is as follows:

Pattern 3.1
Street closure and privatisation (*Figure 3.8*)

(a) **Access on foot and by car to residential streets or groups of streets, should be limited to avoid through movement: e.g. cul-de-sac or return loop layout forms.**
(b) **Any access point should be narrowed and formed as a gateway to symbolise privatisation.**
(c) **Some form of common management or shared legal responsibility for the street is preferred.**

There is not sufficient information from the studies at St Louis and Hartford to state how large these street closures can be but the limit would probably be between fifty and one hundred dwellings. The importance of some socio-legal association being formed to make the closure effective might depend on the location of the streets. In an inner city area with many serious crime problems the need for this would be much greater than in a middle-class suburb with relatively few crime problems.

Neighbourhood patterns and crime
It is only recently that American research has tried to establish how far the physical characteristics of neighbourhoods and extent to which residents employ methods of informal social control contribute to levels of crime. A study of neighbourhoods in Atlanta, Georgia by Stephanie Greenberg, William Rohe and Jay Williams (1981) compared the characteristics of high- and low-crime neighbourhoods. Three pairs of high/

24

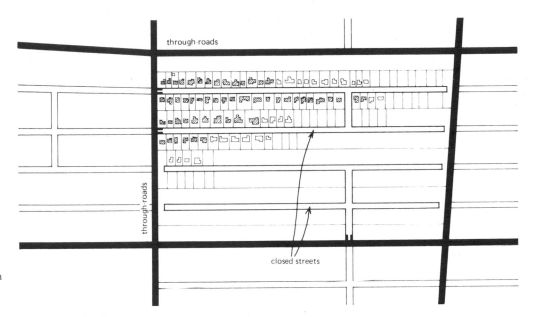

Figure 3.8 Diagrammatic illustration of street closure and privatisation. (Based on Figure 3–15 in Newman, 1973)

low neighbourhoods were selected. Crime levels were based on all reported index crimes. Each pair matched for race and economic status, and they were adjacent, so reducing effects of locational factors. The neighbourhoods were generally residential but excluded public housing. Two of the pairs were black neighbourhoods; one pair was low-income, the other pair was about average for the city. The third pair was of white neighbourhoods with middle- to upper-income levels.

This attempt to produce matched pairs is clearly essential in order to escape the criticisms from criminologists and sociologists who reject design characteristics as contributing to crime, believing that only social and economic factors really matter. Inevitably there were some social differences in the pairs. The mean age was a little higher in the low-crime neighbourhoods than the high-crime neighbourhoods, and the low-income neighbourhoods appear to have a more stable population as the respondents to the survey had been living for a longer period in their present homes. However, many of the social measures showed no significant differences, including education and family composition.

Having satisfied themselves that the neighbourhood pairs were reasonably well matched socially, the authors of this study set about identifying the physical characteristics which differed between the low- and high-crime areas. The simplest way of presenting this is to list these observed differences:
– The proportion of residential property was high in the low-crime neighbourhoods.
– High-crime neighbourhoods had a higher proportion of vacant land.
– Low-crime areas had more single-family dwellings, whereas there were more multi-family units in the high-crime neighbourhoods.
– High-crime neighbourhoods had more major thoroughfares, while low-crime areas had more small neighbourhood streets.
– Development was more homogeneously residential in low-crime neighbourhoods, with a

more mixed land use in high-crime areas.

– Boundaries to high-crime neighbourhoods have more commercial land use and major thoroughfares; low-crime areas appear to have less permeable boundaries with no commercial activity. Most effective seems to be a railroad and possibly an industrial area.

– Neighbourhoods surrounded by areas of lower socio-economic status tended to have a high level of crime.

– Low-crime neighbourhoods had more private parking on private driveways, with less parking on the street or in parking lots.

There is nothing very remarkable about these findings except that this study seems to be the first research to bring these factors together. The findings that crime is more associated with areas with multi-family housing units than single family units would not be surprising to Reppetto (1974) who reported this in *Residential Crime*, one of the earliest major studies. Nor would it be surprising to Newman who had shown such housing forms to be a problem in American public housing (Newman 1973). The increased risk from surrounding areas of lower socio-economic status would also hardly be surprising to any criminologist (Baldwin and Bottoms, 1976).

It must be made quite clear that these findings are merely associative. There is no implication that of themselves these characteristics cause or reduce crime levels. However, it is irresistible to conclude that if these findings were replicable almost anywhere within say western, urban societies, there may be some sense in trying to maximise the conditions known to be associated with less crime and minimise the conditions associated with higher levels of crime.

Together these findings do seem to have implications for planners and neighbourhood developers. The neighbourhoods studied were rather varied in size from under 1000 to nearly 4000 households, but it does seem that if such neighbourhoods can be made more separate and enclosed, more homogeneously residential, more

cut off from main thoroughfares and associated activity, there may be a reduction in crime generally.

The most important patterns which seem to be implied from these findings are as follows:

Pattern 3.2
Homogeneous residential areas

Residential neighbourhoods should be homogeneously developed as housing and not mixed with other uses, particularly commercial uses and vacant land.

Pattern 3.3
Single-family housing preferred building form

Preference should always be given to single-family housing units, and the minimisation of the number of units in any one multi-family structure.

Pattern 3.4
Limit access to neighbourhoods

Access to each residential area of say up to 4000 dwellings should be relatively restricted, certainly by road and probably by pedestrian access. Main routes should not pass through neighbourhoods or even provide their boundaries.

Pattern 3.5
Separation from commercial uses

Residential areas should be kept separate from commercial uses as far as possible.

The most effective forms of separation between neighbourhoods were found to be industrial uses and features such as a railroad. It would seem that any physical barrier which did not generate interaction with the neighbourhood would provide an effective boundary. The diagram in *Figure 3.9* attempts to illustrate these patterns in combination.

At first sight this approach to planning of self-contained neighbourhoods seems to follow the ideas of modern city planning criticised by Christopher Alexander in his award winning

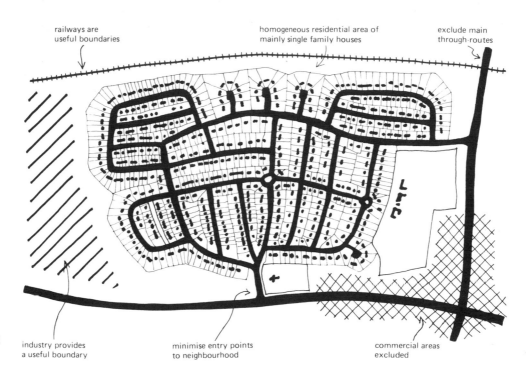

railways are
useful boundaries

homogeneous residential area of
mainly single family houses

exclude main
through-routes

Figure 3.9 Diagram
combining neighbourhood
crime prevention patterns

industry provides
a useful boundary

minimise entry points
to neighbourhood

commercial areas
excluded

article *A City is not a Tree* (Alexander, 1966). His criticism was that planners were designing on the assumption that they were creating self-contained communities, but this was not the reality of modern cities, where social networks formed a lattice-like pattern of relationships. But the crime prevention model here is not aimed at creating self-supporting social entities. Indeed, the social structure of the neighbourhood seems to be unimportant for crime prevention. Greenberg *et al.* found that there were few significant differences between high- and low-crime neighbourhoods in terms of social structure, measured by whether or not friends or relatives live in the same neighbourhood, and the extent to which respondents used local services such as church, doctor, or other medical facility, parks, playground etc.

It might be expected from the writings of Jane Jacobs and Oscar Newman that in the low-crime neighbourhoods people had a stronger sense of territory in that they would be more aware of the presence of strangers and would intervene more readily. However, the evidence from this study was the other way round. There was more evidence from interviews that residents in high-crime neighbourhoods were able to tell strangers from residents, that residents actively watched out for suspicious behaviour, and that they had taken direct action to deal with local problems (e.g. got together with neighbours, called the police or contacted the local authorities).

The purpose of these neighbourhood patterns is, therefore, not to generate any social structure or action as a means of crime control, but simply to manage the patterns of use and movement in a neighbourhood and so reduce the presence of 'outsiders' and others who might be potential offenders.

4 Preventing residential burglary

Burglary is a crime that has received moderate attention from researchers, both in England and Northern America. Harry Scarr (1973) produced a very detailed analysis of *Patterns of Burglary* based on studies of burglary in Washington D.C. and surrounding areas. Scarr's study includes both residential and other burglary such as commercial burglary. Another study was made by Thomas Reppetto (1974) of burglary in the Boston area. It was entitled *Residential Crime* because he also included residential robberies, but burglary dominated his data. These studies are specific to types of crime but they had been planned before Oscar Newman first published his book *Defensible Space* in 1972. They tell us a great deal about burglars and burglary – who are the offenders, the social factors involved, what a burglary offence is like, who the victims are and the role of the criminal justice system. But there is very little on the possibility of prevention of burglary through design.

More recently, useful studies have been made in Canada and England. Irvin Waller and Norman Okihiro (1978) made a detailed study of burglary in Toronto, and Stuart Winchester and Hilary Jackson (1982) made a study in Kent. Both studies took samples of dwellings that had been victimised and dwellings that had not been victimised and both were successful at identifying factors in the design of the environment which appears to contribute to the probability of burglary. The Kent study dealt exclusively with houses.

A further English study has been done by Mike Maguire and Trevor Bennett which makes some useful comparisons between burglary in several different kinds of area – from small town, medium-sized town and a wealthy commuter area within reach of London. Like Scarr, Reppetto, and Waller and Okihiro, Maguire had the advantage of being able to interview burglars serving prison sentences.

The nature of burglary

The meaning of 'burglary' adopted by researchers seems to be very similar in the countries from which research is reported, even though there are legal differences of definition. For example, Waller and Okihiro (1978) point out that there is no legal category of burglary in Canada; the Criminal Code uses 'breaking and entering' as the legal term. Essentially, residential burglary is taken to mean someone entering a private dwelling, without the permission or knowledge of the residents, with the intention of theft or similar action. It normally means breaking in by tampering with a lock, forcing open a door of window or even breaking the glass of a window to gain entry, and may involve entry where there was no force necessary – through a window that was left open or a door left unlocked.

Burglary does not normally involve the use of violence or threat against a victim; this would be classified differently in various countries – such as residential robbery in the USA. In England and Wales there is a category of aggravated burglary which means burglary whilst in possession of a weapon or explosive, but this involves only about 1 in 500 residential burglaries (Home Office, 1981).

There are great difficulties in presenting statistics on crime levels, firstly because of the discrepancies between reported crime and victim survey data. There are also difficulties in comparing different countries because of differences in definitions. However, it does seem worth stating that burglary is a crime that is likely to affect almost everyone. It is a rare event, but as Maguire (1982) puts it, 'the average British citizen can be expected to be burgled twice or three times during his lifetime, calling the police perhaps once'.

From official crime statistics (Home Office, 1980), the risk of burglary taking place in a dwelling in England and Wales during 1980 was 1 in 65. Allowing for the findings of the 1980 General Household Survey on the ratio of reported to unreported residential crime the figure would be about 1 in 40 (25 per 1000 dwellings). This compares closely with the risk in the Toronto study of 1 in 38 (26.4 per 1000 dwellings). Waller and Okihiro were unable to find comparable figures to their own in the United States, but they do quote several rates from central areas of large American cities showing a much greater risk averaging around 130 burglaries per 1000 dwellings (1 in 8).

The general impression is that Canada, as a whole, has a level of burglary similar to or lower than that of Britain and that, although non-metropolitan areas of the USA may have similar rates to Britain, the central areas of large American cities have particularly high rates, probably associated with concentrations of the more disadvantaged sections of the population. This pattern explains the emphasis placed on research in the different countries. The earlier US research emphasised the inner-city problems where high-rise multi-unit housing is common. The UK research includes both rural and small-town areas and concentrates on single-family housing. The Toronto study has some of both aspects but with more emphasis on houses.

As with so much writing and research on crime there is a tendency to treat burglary as a single type of offence. This has the effect of rather obscuring the differences between relatively trivial opportunistic burglary and more carefully considered crimes. Mike Maguire comes closest to building up a more useful picture of the various types of burglary when he looked at burglary in the Thames Valley Police area. The contrasts between burglary in country areas, in small towns, large towns and in wealthy commuter areas are significant and essential to the understanding of prevention. For example, in discussing burglary in Banbury he found that half of the burglaries there occurred in the area of the the town where most of the publicly owned housing is to be found. The evidence from convictions was that many of these burglaries were carried out by local people who were often known to the victims. They involved thefts of cash from near neighbours and a commonly reported offence involved breaking into coin meters which may not have been burglary but 'inside jobs'. Young teenagers and children were often the offenders. There was no way in which the burglars could be regarded as professionals.

In the country area around Banbury, Maguire identifies three general categories. At one extreme there were trivial incidents such as where village children stole food and cash from the houses of people they knew. At the other extreme there were apparently professional thieves who probably travelled from outside the area to take valuable property such as silver and jewellery from wealthy households, including historical country houses. Between these extremes were burglaries by local people who stole cash and electrical goods.

In the case of the professional burglary from wealthy houses, the offenders seem to use little force, often finding access through windows left open or with broken locks. They removed only one or two items which might not have been missed for a day or so. Maguire cites a case where a burglar had entered a cottage through a window but had first removed the Christmas cards and decorations on the window sill. Having emptied a silver cabinet he carefully closed the cabinet and, on leaving through the same window, replaced all the Christmas cards on the window sill.

In his summary of the pattern of burglary in Reading, with a population of 130 000 compared with 30 000 with Banbury, he found it to be dominated by what he describes as 'middle-range' burglary. It involved the taking of cash and electrical equipment including TV sets, implying that in a larger town it is easier to find outlets for stolen goods. Victimised property tended to be in areas either on or near council estates or wealthier than average, the most heavily victimised being high-value properties in the centre or near poorer areas. There was apparently relatively little penetration of large middle-class areas which tended to have burglary confined to their fringes.

A third area studied by Maguire and Bennett was the small town of Gerrards Cross which, although it had a small population of about 8000, was an affluent area. This town, with a high proportion of large houses laid well back from the road and hidden by trees and shrubs, had a rate of burglary of 1 in 25 households, the highest in the Thames Valley area. (The figures are calculated on police data but since most burglaries are higher-value offences it is likely that the report rate would be much higher than the national average.) These were higher-value burglaries with jewellery being taken in over half of the incidents. These burglars were considered by the police to be 'professional criminals'.

As implied by the high figures quoted from central areas of major cities in the United States there is another dimension to the range of burglary that Maguire could not comment on from his data. It is clear that a great deal of inner-city residential burglary is not the work of professional burglars aiming at high rewards. As Waller and Okihiro state: 'From our interviews with incarcerated burglars and our self-report data, we found that in most instances burglary is not an act involving lengthy planning or premeditation but rather one involving the seizure of inviting opportunites by relative amateurs'. Reppetto (1974) indicates that for burglary in the Boston area the offenders who are arrested are disproportionately young, male and non-white. Areas of American cities with large black populations tended to have high burglary rates as did lower-income areas.

The distribution of burglary

This chapter is concerned primarily with the aspects of design which can influence the level of residential burglary, but the main thrust of research on the environmental factors in burglary has been in its distribution. It seems well worth summarising the main distributional characteristics of the crime if for no other reason than that it helps to locate those places where most attention should be given to design prevention.

It is clear from what has already been stated that residential burglary is largely associated with urban areas. In rural areas there is probably little cause for concern over burglary except in the case of isolated valuable property and country houses. Small towns similarly have a relatively minor burglary problem, but at least, in Britain, burglary of a relatively minor nature does seem to become concentrated in areas of public housing estates. Where there are small towns or villages within easy reach of large urban areas which are well established wealthy commuter areas they may act as attractive targets for the more 'professional' burglar (see Maguire on Gerrards Cross, 1982).

As the urban area becomes larger so the burglary rate increases. It is clear that generalisation can easily be taken too far, but there does seem to be some general pattern that can be seen in studies in USA, Canada, England and New Zealand. There are three main components of this pattern:

1 Poor areas

In England Maguire (1982) has identified the influence on distribution by the presence of local authority housing estates even in quite small urban areas. Nearness to public sector housing was also found to be a factor influencing the victimisation rate of houses, though not of apartments, in Toronto (Waller and Okihiro, 1978). In the United States, public housing seems to be regarded as being associated with concentrations of higher burglary rates, but research has emphasised the association with non-white and low-income neighbourhoods as well as rented tenure. As Reppetto (1974) points out:

'the statistical association between the crime rate and the racial composition of the neighborhood may only reflect negative correlation between income and percent non-white, with income being the causal variable in the determination of residential crime'.

The main reason for this association seems to be that offenders, who tend to be from poor areas, travel relatively short distances to commit burglary. This was shown in Reppetto's study of Boston and in a more general way by Baldwin and Bottoms (1976) in their studies of Sheffield. Davidson (1981: 67–69) summarises this and other work in United States and his own in Christchurch, New Zealand. This short distance travelled is particularly the case for the young, more opportunistic burglar. Travel distance increases for the older and more 'professional' burglar.

2 Urban core areas

There is a fairly general pattern, particularly in large cities, for the central area to have high rates of burglary. This was shown clearly in the Boston study by Reppetto (1974) who found that the annual rate of burglary in the core area of Boston was 39 per 1000 dwellings; adjacent to the core the rate was 22 per 1000, and the outlying areas studied had an average rate of only 12 per 1000. This pattern was also found in Toronto (Waller and Okihiro 1978; see Appendix B). The reasons for this pattern are certain to be complex. Partly it will be due to the frequent existence of poor run-down inner-city areas which are also mixed with higher-value property areas.

Another factor which is often presented by researchers is the degree of social cohesion based on the extent to which people had lived in the neighbourhood, knew their neighbours and felt they helped each other. In areas which scored low degrees of social cohesion Reppetto found the average annual rate of residential burglary to be 90 per 1000 dwellings compared with 28 and 16 per 1000 for areas with medium and high levels of social cohesion.

Generally it seems that areas of rental housing with a mainly transient population are associated with a higher level of residential burglary and also tend to be located in the older, inner areas of large cities. The area of Christchurch with the most burglary was described by Davidson (1981:41) as a 'zone in transition'. Waller and Okihiro found that higher percentages of households with lodgers were associated with higher burglary rates (1978:51).

3 Wealthy housing

Although this is less significant than the two other components, there does seem evidence in both the Canadian and English studies that wealthy housing creates an attraction to the more professional burglar. Maguire's example of Gerrards Cross has been mentioned. Waller and Okihiro refer to the existence of one or two affluent pockets of suburban Toronto which had higher rates. The study of burglary in Kent (Jackson and Winchester, 1982) showed that high rateable value of property increased the risk of burglary. Baldwin and Bottoms (1976) showed that property with a rateable value of over £200 in Sheffield had an annual rate of burglary of 52 per 1000 dwellings compared with an average rate for the city of 7 burglaries per 1000 in a year.

These patterns of distribution of burglary can be summarised diagrammatically, with the presentation of the distribution of higher burglary risk shown for an imaginary urban area in *Figure 4.1.*

pockets of
wealthy housing

public
housing

typical distribution of
incidents of burglary

Figure 4.1 Typical distribution of burglary in a major city

Residential building form

In the early writing on crime and the designed environment, the impression is given that crime is most associated with modern multi-unit and high-rise housing schemes (Jacobs, 1962; Newman, 1972). It was also mentioned in Chapter 3 that high-crime areas tended to have multi-family dwellings rather than single-family houses.

In Reppetto's Boston study, partly in response to Newman's book which was published while Reppetto was still writing, he tried to analyse his data to test Newman's contention that large-scale buildings tended to have more crime. He classified his reporting areas by the predominant housing type. The results are shown in *Table 4.1*. The use of the category 'public housing projects' reflects the fact that such areas were seen as sufficiently different from the others to justify a separate analysis, which no doubt is the nature of public housing projects in major cities in the United States.

The data supports the idea that multi-family structures are most associated with burglary. Reppetto also pointed out that, if the luxury high-rise areas were excluded from the analysis, the burglary rate for areas with predominantly large multi-family structures would rise to 57

per 1000 dwellings per annum. However, it is quite likely that such an analysis is misleading. Structure type may be related to crime through other social factors which are known to relate to crime occurring in association with building type. Reppetto gives a correlation matrix which shows that building form is correlated to some degree with income levels and crime level in neighbouring areas, which in turn are correlated with social differences. It could mean simply that higher burglary rate and multi-family housing

TABLE 4.1 Burglary rates in areas of different housing types in Boston

Predominant type of housing in area	Average residential burglary rate per 1000 dwelling units
Single-family structures	14
Small multi-unit structures 2-9 units (usually walk-up)	30
Public housing projects	34
Large multi-family structures 10 or more units (often elevator buildings)	37

Source: Reppetto (1974) Table 3-8, published with permission.

are both associated with similar social factors, without the latter causing the former in any way.

Reppetto also presented further interesting data which shows something of the variations within burglary. He showed slides of several housing forms to a sample of ninety-seven incarcerated burglars and asked them to indicate in which type they most frequently operated. The results are shown in *Table 4.2*.

TABLE 4.2 Types of housing preferred by burglars

Type of housing	Per cent of burglars
Single-family houses	35
Small multi-family houses (known locally locally as three- or four-deckers)	28
Public housing project with elevator buildings	19
Large multi-unit older brick apartment buildings	8
Attached (row) houses	6
Luxury high-rise apartment buildings	4

Source: Reppetto (1974) part of Table 2-4, published with permission.

The preference for burglary of single-family houses was greatest among the older burglars (over 25), whereas young burglars (under 18) selected mainly multi-family houses and public housing projects. These findings follow the pattern described by Maguire (1982) in England with younger burglars operating in and around council housing areas and the older more professional burglars selecting the more affluent houses. Reppetto's interviews revealed that the older burglars gave apparent affluence as the principal reason for their choice of target, whereas the younger burglars gave ease of access as the main reason for their choice.

Accessibility is almost certainly the key issue. It is probably not the form of the housing as such but the ease of access in any particular case that

makes it vulnerable to burglary. Recent work by Newman and Franck (1980) produces clear findings on this issue based on interviews of residents on sixty-three federally-assisted urban housing developments in the United States. They developed measures for the design variables in 'building size' and 'accessibility' and as part of a more general analysis correlated them with burglary. Their measure of building size was a combination of the number of apartment units that share a building entry and the building type (row house, walk-ups and without gallery access and high rise). Building size did not correlate with burglary (-0.05) but accessibility did 0.43).

The conclusion from this should be that, from the point of view of burglary prevention, it is not the general form of the building that influences burglary rate but its accessibility. The reasons why high-rise and other multi-unit forms of housing have been considered to suffer from higher burglary rates are that they tend to be built in places where the burglary rate is high – in the inner areas of cities, in low-income districts and particularly in public housing. It is probably for these reasons that fear of crime and what Newman and Franck call 'instability', the tendency for high turnover, vacancy and the desire of tenants to move out, were found to correlate quite strongly with building size.

The prevention of burglary

Burglary is generally regarded by researchers as an opportunistic crime, with rather more planning in the case of burglary from wealthy property. Maguire (1980) uses the term 'sought opportunity' to distinguish the idea of opportunistic in the sense of spontaneous action on the stimulus of seeing some opportunity. The evidence points to individuals deliberately seeking opportunities to burgle.

In the case of most residential burglary, the rewards are generally modest and this is probably the main reason why it is a non-violent crime; it would not be worth the risk of using violence and it is therefore avoided as far as possible. Those who take up burglary rather than other crimes may be showing preference for non-violent methods. All the burglar is seeking, is to gain access and slip away again without the occupants knowing and without raising the suspicions of neighbours or others who might intervene or call the police. Most burglars will try and avoid any form of confrontation.

The most obvious proof of the desire to avoid contact with the occupants of a dwelling is the fact that most burglaries occur in unoccupied dwellings. Reppetto (1974) found that in areas where 60% or more of dwellings were unoccupied during the daytime for more than 35 hours per week, the rate of burglaries was more than three times that of other areas in Boston. Waller and Okihiro (1978) found that dwellings were much more likely to be victimised if they were unoccupied for more than 47 hours per week. Thirty per cent of houses that were burgled were in this low occupancy category compared with only 16% of non-burgled houses. They found that occupancy also influenced the choice of apartments but to a lesser extent. The figures for apartments were 69% and 42% respectively. Jackson and Winchester (1982:21) found in their Kent study that 80% of the victimised houses had been unoccupied at the time.

It is this factor of occupancy which distinguishes the pattern of residential and non-residential burglary. Scarr's (1973) study investigated both residential and non-residential burglary. There were marked differences in the time of day that residential and non-residential burglary occurred. *Table 4.3* shows the percentages for burglaries occurring in the daytime and night-time in residential and non-residential accommodation taken from Scarr's study of the Washington area.

It is clear from this that residential burglary is more likely to occur during the day than at night, whereas non-residential burglary is more likely to take place at night. Scarr also found that the hours from 10.00 to 16.00 were the

main daylight hours for residential burglary. Although there are variations in emphasis, the findings of Waller and Okihiro and Jackson and Winchester all show that residential burglary occurs most frequently in the daytime. The reason for this time pattern is that dwellings are most often left alone during the day than at night whereas commercial property is usually unoccupied at night.

The fact that residential burglary occurs mainly in the daytime when houses and apartments are unoccupied has implications for design and management of the environment. It opens up the

TABLE 4.3 Percentage of burglaries occurring during day/night time

	1967	1968	1969
Residential burglary			
night	45	45	50
night	27	34	26
unknown	28	21	24
Non-residential burglary			
day	10	9	6
night	51	53	56
unknown	39	38	38

Source: Scarr (1973) Table 21.

possibility of surveillance both by neighbours and people such as caretakers and doormen in apartment buildings. Brief reference was made to the problems of evaluating street lighting in Chapter 2. It is clear from these findings that street lighting is not particularly relevant to residential burglary, which is more likely to happen in broad daylight. However, the situation is quite different for commercial and industrial premises where burglary is more of a night-time phenomenon. The claims of the lighting industry in relation to non-residential security may be justified, but less so for residential use risk.

Theoretical model of prevention
Drawing on the findings of Waller (1978, 1979) and Maguire (1982), which were influenced by

interviews with convicted burglars, and the work by Jackson and Winchester (1982), a theoretical model emerges which gives more emphasis to the location, setting and general layout of housing than to conventional security measures. An intending burglar will first choose an area of housing depending on habitual pattern – silver and jewellery from wealthy property, consumer electric goods from middle-class housing, or just speculative attempt to obtain money from his own neighbourhood. The intruder then selects individual houses or even groups of houses which seem likely to be unoccupied, and which provide easy access to potential entry points without much risk of being seen making an entry (hidden by shrubs, at back of house, a more isolated house, etc).

Having selected a house, it can be checked for occupancy by visual evidence or, as Maguire found, by calling at the house to see if anyone answers the door. Only when the house is found to be empty does the next stage of defeating security measures begin. The nature of locks and other measures used on windows and doors can only be discovered by the intending burglar at this point. Having committed himself thus far, the security measures would have to be exceptional to prevent a determined burglar. If doors and windows have not been left insecure, they can usually be forced open or a window broken.

A house which provides entry points that are free from surveillance by neighbours or passers-by is clearly more vulnerable to attack because the process of breaking in can be relatively leisurely. The only burglars who would be deterred are those who rely on access through windows and doors left insecure – the type of burglary most associated with poorer housing and problematic public housing.

This model assumes a degree of social cohesion in that neighbours and other passers-by would call the police, or intervene themselves, if they saw a stranger behaving in a suspicious way. Waller and Okihiro (1978) found to some extent that victimised households reported a lower level of social cohesion than non-victimised houses. Their measure was based on favourable responses to questions such as: how long they had lived there, whether they knew their neighbours' names or whether they were close friends and would they take in a parcel etc. For houses they found that 62% of victims compared with 45% of non-victims reported low social cohesion. The findings were less clear for apartments but, if anything, suggested that the opposite was true. Apartment residents appear more socially isolated.

This suggests that the model may be most relevant to houses rather than apartment housing. Waller and Okihiro did find that occupancy rates for apartments were less influential on burglary rate than for houses. This may be because it is more difficult for the intending burglar to tell at a distance whether an apartment is unoccupied. Also, since the access areas to apartment doors cannot so easily be supervised it would be easier for intending burglars to try many doors on a more speculative basis. As will be seen, the best line of defence for apartments is to keep potential burglars out of the building altogether.

The patterns that are required for design and management of housing are presented in the following sections. It will be seen that the issues relating to burglary prevention in multi-dwelling structures are different from those for houses, whether the houses are single detached houses or terraced row houses.

Large-scale planning implications

Undoubtedly these are rather speculative patterns, compared with the smaller-scale patterns, but they do tie burglary in to the ideas presented in the chapter on Neighbourhood Patterns.

The first question is: how serious an issue for the planner is the fact that nearness to subsidised public housing is a factor in burglary? The Toronto study data are rather unclear in that the category 'near to public subsidised housing' not only referred to respondents living within a few blocks of a housing project but also included those living in such housing. Nevertheless, the study found that more than half the victims were in this category compared with only 12% of the non-victims (Waller and Okihiro 1978: 59). As they point out this may not identify public housing to be the cause itself, as such housing (in North America) is usually found in areas that are low in socio-economic status etc.

However, this relationship to public housing also emerges in Maguire's study of Reading (and to a lesser extent the smaller town of Banbury). He found that burglaries were more likely to occur where wealthy homes and poor homes are situated in close proximity, and middle-class housing suffered more burglary in areas adjacent to poorer housing. These patterns were mostly associated with the location of council housing estates.

Further support for this pattern of adjacency comes from earlier work by Paul and Patricia Brantingham (1975) who made an analysis of the distribution of burglary in Tallahassee, Florida. They constructed a computer model of the city to generate 'perceptually homogeneous neighbourhood sets' from variables such as race, property values, rent and percentage of single- or multiple-family dwellings. They found that boundary blocks – those adjacent to boundaries between homogeneous sets – had higher burglary rates than interior blocks. These findings suggest that property in more mixed or transitional zones is more likely to be selected by burglars. It is very similar to Maguire's comment on Reading that 'offenders were unwilling to penetrate too deeply into exclusively middle-class areas on the outskirts of the town, concentrating chiefly upon houses close to the main roads'.

If burglary prevention was the only criterion for urban planning, the evidence above, such as it is, points to the minimisation of mixed or heterogeneous housing areas and the maximisation of the size of homogeneous housing areas, or put more simply:

Pattern 4.1
Location of poorer housing

Areas of wealthy or middle-class/middle-income housing should be separated as far as possible from poorer housing.

Such a pattern may be unacceptable to planners and politicians but it is consistent with the notions of the neighbourhood patterns in Chapter 3, both on the idea of minimal access to neighbourhoods and that neighbourhoods should be socio-economically homogeneous. What is also interesting is that the natural pressures of movement such as the 'flight to the suburbs' by the middle-class whites in the United States and the development of 'exclusive' areas of wealthier housing around most major Western European cities suggests that many would believe in this pattern.

Apartment buildings
For guidance on apartments and all multi-unit structures we have to rely mainly on North American research. If Reppetto's interviews of burglars were reliable, the problem in large buildings is to prevent the younger burglar who, as has been suggested, is more opportunistic. The exception to this may be the luxury apartment building where the older more professional burglar could be interested.

Newman's original presentation of 'defensible space' (1972) was directed mainly at multi-unit housing on public housing projects. Although burglary does not appear to be an important element in the defensible space argument it is reasonable to assume that the ideas of increasing residents' territorial control of their blocks and encouraging natural surveillance would be relevant to burglary in so far as they discourage access to the buildings within the projects by intending burglars. However, there was no specific evidence in the original research to suggest any one form of building is less at risk from burglary than any other.

In their research in Toronto, Waller and Okihiro gave some thought to trying to test Newman's theory but they sum up their efforts as follows:

'Our findings for apartments question the conclusions drawn from the "defensible space" literature. The location of the apartment in the building, affluence, and the presence of a doorman were much more important factors in determining the likelihood of victimisation than items such as social cohesion'.

They go on to say

'Our findings suggest that strategies of restricting entry in apartments are a particularly effective means of preventing burglary'.

Perhaps more realistic therefore are Newman's more recent ideas in his study with Karen Franck (1980). Since they showed that their measures for accessibility correlated well with burglary it is worth summarising these measures for multi-unit housing, as they could be regarded as a rough guideline to security practice for public housing apartment blocks.

The scaling used was divided into walk-ups and high-rises. The features considered as contributing equally to the total score for *walk-ups* were:

1 *Apartment doors easily visible* from the street or from the windows of apartment buildings opposite.
2 *A lock on the front common entry door* to the apartment building.
3 *Front door kept locked* on at least 50% of buildings in a project.
4 *Inaccessible front windows* on the ground floor or along the access gallery. Three conditions qualify as inaccessible:
(a) cannot be reached without ladder;
(b) area next to windows is enclosed by a real barrier;

(c) the windows are narrow metal-framed louvred windows or have metal guards.
5 *Inaccessible rear windows* on the ground floor. The same conditions as in 4 apply here.

For *high-rises* the measures were scored from the three following conditions:

1 *Doors with locks* for both front common entrance and secondary exits.
2 *Secondary exits kept locked.*
3 *Common front door kept locked with intercom system,* or a guard on duty when door not locked.

Entries to apartment
It is clear that, for apartments other than at ground level, one important line of defence is the common front access point to the apartment block, providing also that any secondary or exit doors are kept locked. The Boston and Toronto studies showed that the use of doormen or security guards was highly effective in deterring burglars; even though they are normally associated with more affluent developments which in theory would be more attractive, at least to the older burglar. Burglars appear to avoid the risk of personal confrontation, as it has been found that unmanned alternatives to doormen or security guards are far less effective.
Waller and Okihiro (1978:62) state:

'None of the victimised apartment buildings employed a doorman. When we compared the proportions of victimised apartments having working intercom systems with non-victimised apartments, a slight and statistically insignificant effect was noticed. Victims were marginally less likely to have working intercom systems. This suggests that these systems function to screen visitors and intending burglars to some limited extent, but not as efficiently as doormen'.

An alternative of using TV surveillance systems is often proposed in security literature, and such systems have been used to improve security of apartment buildings. Musheno, Levine and Palumbo (1978), cited in Rubenstein *et al.* (1980), reported on the use of cameras in the lobbies and elevators of blocks containing fifty-three apartments. The pictures transmitted by the cameras could be viewed by residents on their own TV screens by selecting the appropriate channel. After three months of installation the experiment was considered a failure. Few tenants used the system regularly, no tenant had observed criminal activity on TV, and there was no significant change in crime rates, even though more than 1200 apartments were involved.

An interesting 'pioneering installation' in four 19-storey blocks of flats in the London Borough of Hammersmith has been reported by Mary Smith (1980). (A follow-up article appeared in 1982.) Here a television-linked entry-phone system was installed only after more simple systems had been in use. Originally an entry-phone system was introduced which had not been satisfactory, 'because of poor design and misuse of the equipment by some of the tenants. This resulted in vandalism and nuisance in the entrance halls . . . , frequent burglaries, general dissatisfaction and loss of confidence by residents'. Vacancies were about 7%.

Improvements were made which involved strengthening various parts of the system, such as stronger push-button panels, encasing wires, strengthening doors and door-release mechanisms. This resulted in some reduction of vandalism but damage to internal doors, walls and lifts continued, especially after the caretakers had gone off duty at 21.00 hours. A further measure was then added after a trial in one block which involved the use of a TV system that could be viewed on tenants' own TV screens and by the estate caretaker. Cameras were sited to view the entrance to each block from inside through the wire glass entry doors. This facility meant that tenants could see who was calling on the entry-phone and caretakers either saw or received reports from tenants about nuisance and loiterers, and could speak to potential intruders. A

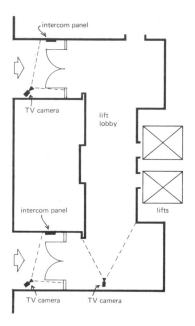

Figure 4.2 A plan of the entrance to Poynter House on the Edward Woods Estate, Hammersmith, in which a more developed system has been installed. TV cameras cover both entry doors and lift waiting areas. Door locks are magnetic and can be operated remotely or by electronically programmed proximity cards. There is no mechanical locking hardware to damage

reduction in burglary was reported as well as increased tenant involvement in the general care of the blocks.

It would seem from this that, if there is to be effective security against potential burglars at the entry to an apartment block, there must be

Figure 4.3 The TV monitor in the caretaker's flat or the TV sets of tenants relay pictures of both entry doors and lift lobby on a split screen. The caretaker also has a control panel to speak to any location. It also warns him if any doors have jammed open. (Photo published with permission of London Borough of Hammersmith and Fulham)

the potential for human intervention and therefore a real risk of confrontation. The pattern required might be defined as:

Pattern 4.2
Entrances to apartment buildings

The common entrances to an apartment building must be either manned by doormen or similar security personnel, or kept locked with the potential of human surveillance through electronic means. The human element should include resident management or caretaking staff.

As more experience is gained with these more developed forms of entry-phone systems, it will be possible to define their effectiveness more precisely. It would be interesting to see what adaptations potential burglars might develop. The Hammersmith scheme, for example, has a provision for delivery men to enter the building by pushing a special button which operates the doors between 6.30 and 13.30 hours. Anyone knowing of the button could gain access between these times. Similarly the self-closing mechanisms on the doors are slow enough to allow the use of prams and pushchairs. It would not be difficult for an intending burglar to slip in through the doors as a tenant is leaving. Perhaps the risk of being seen remains a sufficient deterrent.

In *Design Guidelines for Creating Defensible Space* (1976) Newman draws attention to the problem of the economics of lifts and doormen; both are costly. The most economic solution would be a high-rise apartment block served by one bank of lifts and looked after by one doorman. Newman suggests that if the provision of a doorman is not possible, a solution which divides the building into a series of separate access systems would be preferable. It would seem likely that the alternative in pattern 4.2 of entry-phone plus electronic surveillance would suit this multi-access building form.

One of the difficulties of trying to set out ideas on burglary prevention in a reasonably comprehensive way is that there are so many research questions which remain to be studied. For example, the idea in Newman's guidelines of dividing walk-up blocks into several access systems (Newman 1976:82). Is it really necessary to use an entry-phone? If so, would that be sufficient or would some form of electronic surveillance be necessary? The answers do not exist. So much depends on the location of the building and the income levels of the residents.

Newman did not address himself to the problem of what, in Britain, are called 'deck-access designs'. These are where the access corridors in a number of apartment blocks are joined end-to-end by short walkways between blocks creating routes through housing projects at many levels extending several hundred metres. With frequent vertical access points, projects containing many hundreds of dwellings are totally publicly accessible. Attempts are now being made to create locked zones which give tenants access only to their own zones to reduce the extent of access by potential offenders. It will be interesting to see how effective such zones are without some human surveillance element in the system.

Doors to apartments
If pattern 4.2 for entrance doors to apartment buildings cannot be provided for economic reasons, the next line of defence must be the door to the individual apartment. Where the windows of an apartment are inaccessible (or perhaps 'hardened' in the manner of the measures used by Newman and Franck, 1980), there is some evidence from Reppetto's work that the quality of the door to an apartment can influence burglary risk. Reppetto categorised the dwellings in his survey of Boston into those protected by good standard doors and those of poorer 'non-standard' quality. He found that the average annual rate of burglaries through the door of a dwelling was 81 per 1000 dwellings with non-standard doors, but with the better

quality 'standard' door, the rate dropped to 28 per 1000. The improvement was most noticeable in the high-crime areas where most of the dwellings (91%) were in multi-unit structures; the rate through 'non-standard' doors was 105 but for 'standard' doors it was only 17 per 1000 dwellings. The required pattern is:

Pattern 4.3
Doors to apartments

The doors to apartments should be strongly constructed with a good locking system. Any surrounding structure should be at least as strong as the door (e.g. avoid use of delivery hatches next to the door or glazed top lights over the entrance doors).

This pattern will be most effective where apartment windows are inaccessible or otherwise protected. However, the pattern would be of value in all apartment buildings. It seems absurd to reduce the protection on the door simply because the apartment was not protected as well elsewhere.

The definition of 'standard' door adopted by Reppetto may be of interest to those wishing to specify an adequate door for this pattern. It must:

1 be of metal, metal panels, solid wood or hollow wood at least three-quarters of an inch thickness (18 mm);
2 have no unprotected glass near the door handle;
3 have no exposed hinges;
4 lock with either a three-quarter inch (18 mm) dead latch or dead bolt or vertical bolt.

From the research design by Reppetto there is no way of knowing which of these characteristics are most important.

It is not claimed that burglars will not be able to defeat a 'standard' door, but that in the context of an apartment building, a good quality door will take a burglar more time than a flimsy door or a lock that can be easily forced. There is

always some risk that he will be seen or heard at work by another resident. If it is the case that burglars will not attempt to enter where there is a risk of being seen or heard at work, a logical extention of this pattern would be:

Pattern 4.4
Arrangement of apartment doors

Doors to apartments should not be isolated from areas used by other residents, but grouped in lobbies serving several apartments. Spy-holes in doors would probably contribute to a potential burglar's perceived risk.

Newman's book *Defensible Space* cites the lobbies in the Brownsville Houses as an illustration of a design that encourages tenants to extend their territorial control beyond the confines of their apartment (see *Figure 4.4*). Some might dispute this concept of territorial control, as has been said in Chapter 2, but there is little doubt that the lobbies are a good illustration of this pattern.

Houses
The patterns for designing against burglary that are presented in the rest of this chapter are derived from four sources already mentioned: the Toronto study by Waller and Okihiro (1978), the study of factors influencing crime in public housing in the USA by Newman and Franck (1980), the recent book on burglary in the Thames Valley police area by Mike Maguire (1982), and the Home Office study of burglary in Kent (Jackson and Winchester, 1982). It is important to acknowledge that these studies, apart from being made in different locations, deal with different types of housing stock. The Newman and Franck study dealt only with public housing whereas the Home Office study had very little public-sector housing.

For the most part the two English studies did not include large urban areas; the largest town in Maguire's study had a population of 130 000 whereas the Newman and Franck study was

40

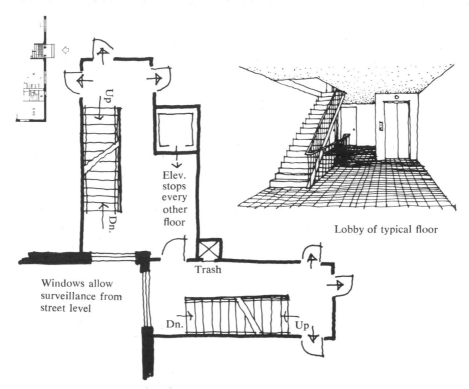

Lobby of typical floor

Elev. stops every other floor

Up

Dn.

Trash

Windows allow surveillance from street level

Dn.

Up

Figure 4.4 Newman's illustration of lobbies in Brownsville Buildings (from Newman, (1972). (Reproduced by permission)

confined to cities of 150 000–750 000 population. Toronto has a population of over a million. These population differences must be relevant to problems of crime prevention because it is known that burglary rates are higher in large urban areas, but it is impossible from the research so far available to know how these differences affect the validity of the patterns that are proposed. Patterns which appear to be effective in small towns, suburban and semi-rural areas may well be overwhelmed by other factors in an inner area of a large conurbation, or on a public housing estate where there are major social and economic problems. We can but hope that research will continue and that we will have better insight into the locational differences.

General house patterns
The following three patterns probably apply to all types of house design and layout. Already in

Chapter 3 on safe neighbourhood design, a pattern was defined which suggested that residential areas should not have principal roads passing through them (pattern 3.4). From two of the burglary studies comes the specific observation that houses close to or on main roads are more likely to be burgled. Maguire (1982) notes that this was the case in the town of Banbury. He also observed that burglars at Reading concentrated on middle-class houses close to main roads. Jackson and Winchester (1982) found that victimised houses in towns were more likely to be on busy through-roads.

These observations fit well with the model of burglary prevention in that properties are chosen at a distance. Clearly houses on main streets are more likely to be noticed by potential burglars than in side streets, or perhaps the potential offender will look at houses in main streets as he is less likely to be noticed as a stranger or as

41

someone acting suspiciously. It is quite conceivable that housing layouts can be designed to avoid houses facing onto main thoroughfares; indeed in contemporary planning terms this might be seen as a benefit for safer road design, allowing access from houses only on minor side streets.

Pattern 4.5
Houses and through-routes

Houses should not face onto main through-roads, and should preferably not be easily visible from such routes. Houses should face onto and be accessed only from side roads. (see *Figure 4.5*).

The next pattern is concerned with surveillance of houses by neighbours and others using the neighbourhood. It is perhaps the most classic remnant of Newman's theory of defensible space. In the Toronto study, Waller and Okihiro (1978:56) measured the surveillability of the houses with a four-point scale for each side of the house that was accessible. The scaling took into account the distance back from the street or to the next house on either side and the nature of visual obstructions (walls, hedges etc.). A total score for each house was the average for all accessible sides. The results were that 59% of victimised houses were found to be coded as difficult to supervise (a score of less than 2.5) compared with only 36% for non-victimised houses.

This finding is reflected in the two English studies. In the Thames Valley study, comments are made that the wealthy houses on large plots with good cover from shrubs and trees were more victimised, as were houses victimised in the Kent study that were more distant from neighbouring houses. These homes also had gardens which were not overlooked and obscured from public view by trees, shrubs, fences and by virtue of being a long way back from the road.

42

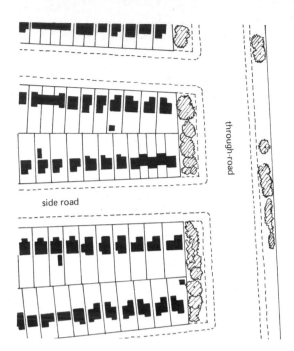

side road

through-road

Figure 4.5 Houses should not face onto main through-roads – Pattern 4.5

Pattern 4.6
Surveillability of houses

Accessible sides of houses should be relatively open and unobstructed by walls, trees or other landscape and they should be close to the street and to other houses which overlook them.

Waller and Okihiro (1978) found that houses in areas of greater social cohesion had a better chance of not being victimised, although the differences were not statistically significant. It can be assumed that surveillance is most effective in socially cohesive neighbourhoods. In this study the scale used to measure social cohesion was based on answers to questions on the length of time residents had lived there, how well they knew their neighbours, how often they spoke to them, if they knew their names, whether or not they would take in a parcel for them etc.

The previous pattern (4.5) is concerned with the surveillance of accessible sides of the houses.

Figure 4.6 Wealthy houses on large plots with good cover from shrubs, trees and walls were more victimised in the Kent study. (Photo by author)

Figure 4.7 These houses illustrate pattern 4.6. Only the fronts of these houses are accessible and they are completely open to surveillance from houses opposite and from anyone using the roadway. Access to the rear is only via a locked or bolted gate. (Photo by author)

One way to deal with areas which are difficult to survey by neighbours and others using the neighbourhood is to limit access, particularly to the back of the house. Maguire notes his belief that this was true of some of the houses in Banbury which suffered less from burglary. Jackson and Winchester (1982) also found in their Kent study that houses with access to the back of the house on both sides of the house were more likely to be victimised. These findings suggest that the risk of burglary is reduced when the following pattern is present:

Pattern 4.7
Access to rear of house

There should be no open access from the front to the rear of a house. Access might be restricted to full height locked gates.

It is not made clear from the studies what barrier would be adequate but the assumptions which Newman and Franck used are probably sufficient. A 6 ft (1.8 m) wall is high enough to make the action of climbing it draw the attention of neighbours as a suspicious behaviour. It may also offer more risk to the intruder since he cannot be certain that no one is on the other side able to observe him. According to the theoretical model presented earlier in the chapter, if an intending burglar calls at the front door to check that the house is empty, he will hope for the minimum of resistance to slipping round to the back of the house once he has found no answer. Also, access all round the house will make escape easier should a neighbour happen to see him and come round to investigate.

In combination, the two patterns 4.6 and 4.7 suggest that the common arrangement of open-

Figure 4.8 Pattern 4.7 is common in English suburban housing, where the fronts are left open, or relatively open, but the gaps between houses are filled in with garages or full height gates or fencing. Rear gardens usually have high fences or walls. (Photo by author)

Figure 4.9 Pattern 4.7 is frequently omitted from suburban housing in the United States, as in this example from Maryland. (Photo by author)

plan fronts to houses, relatively free of screening landscape, with a rear garden or yard completely enclosed by a high fence or wall, is a sound form for design against burglary. Furthermore, to plan houses fairly close together and so that they face one another across a street, all contributes to secure design (*Figure 4.10*).

These principles of security would be best represented by terraced (or row) housing where there is no access to the back gardens or yards. Not only is access around the side of the house impossible but also the sides are inaccessible. Also the closeness of the next house will provide good surveillance from next door of both those who approach the front of a house and those who gain access to the rear garden or yard. Remarkably strong evidence to demonstrate the security of terraced or row housing comes from the Jackson and Winchester study. They calculated from their data on victims and non-victims that the risk of burglary in a detached house was 1 in 29 but for semi-detached houses and short terraces the risk was only 1 in 209. For long terraces the risk was as small as 1 in 540.

It is important to qualify such findings. It would be wrong to assume that any terraced house would be safer than a detached house. Generally the data were drawn from suburban and rural areas. The character of the designs would be quite different from a Georgian square in London. More important is the fact that detached houses represent (particularly in Britain) a higher-income group owner. It is very clear from Maguire (1982), and from the Toronto study, that more affluent housing does attract more burglary. Nevertheless, the difference in rates of burglary between terraced or row houses and detached houses must be partly accounted for by physical design differences.

Because of these differences, it is worth making one or two separate points about row houses and detached houses. Newman and Franck's study of public housing, which produced a clear correlation between accessibility and burglary, included row houses in the analysis, and it is worth quoting the criteria for accessibility that produced the correlation. Unlike the walk-ups and high-rises the scoring was simply 0–3 for

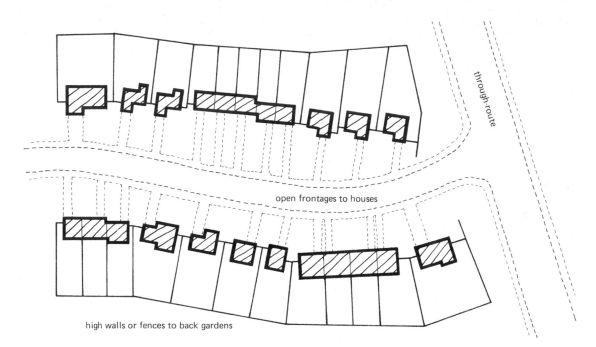

open frontages to houses

high walls or fences to back gardens

through-route

Figure 4.10 Diagrammatic representation of patterns 4.6 and 4.7 combined. This is very similar to the form of housing shown in Figure 4.7

completely accessible to completely inaccessible ground-floor windows. Completely inaccessible windows were either facing onto an area enclosed by a 'real barrier at least six feet high', or the windows were narrow metal-framed louvred windows, or the windows were provided with guards. The next most secure category (score 2) was where either front or back windows conformed to these requirements. They gave a score of 1 to houses with front windows facing the street but the grounds next to the back window enclosed only by a symbolic barrier (e.g. a low wall). The lowest score of zero went to houses which were fully accessible front and back.

From this limited evidence it would seem worth stiffening the requirement of pattern 4.7 in the case of row or terraced houses, particularly where they are in poorer housing districts.

Pattern 4.8
Accessibility to row/terrace houses

(a) **The back garden or yard of a terraced house should be surrounded by a 6 ft (1.8 m) high fence or wall unless the windows are guarded.**
(b) **If the above conditions are not possible at the front of the house it should at least face the street (see also pattern 4.6).**

Figure 4.11 The risk of burglary in terraced or row houses has been found to be much smaller than for detached houses. (Photo by author)

Detached houses for higher-income groups
It is not possible to say much specifically about
the design of houses designed for higher-income
groups, which have relatively large plots and
ample space between houses. The value of surveillance in a less compact housing layout is
clearly reduced and with large plot sizes, it is less
likely that owners would avoid trees and shrubs
growing up over the years to produce considerable screening. However, patterns 4.5, 4.6 and
4.7 would perhaps contribute some protection.

The most satisfactory layout for larger detached housing seems to be a conventional
arrangement of plots always bounded by other
gardens or inaccessible land uses. The Kent
study seems to have found that houses were
more victimised if 'not adjacent to gardens of
other houses but next to some other land use,
particularly privately owned open land such as
farmland'.

Pattern 4.9
Layout of plots for large detached houses

**Plots with large detached houses are best plan-
ned adjacent to each other or to inaccessible land
and not adjacent to open land.**

It has to be constantly stressed that the definitions of these patterns will continue to develop.
For example, Waller and Okihiro came to believe from their pilot interviews that publicly
accessible land bordering on a house was likely
to increase the risk of burglary, as is suggested
by the pattern above. However, the main study
revealed no effect from the presence of a path-
way, park, ravine, school or factory next to the
house. Of course, another study of different
design might conclude very differently. Similar
findings are in conflict in other studies. Maguire
believed that, in the wealthy housing of Gerrards
Cross, the risk was greater to corner houses
(maybe this made escape easier if the intruder
was distrubed) but Waller and Okihiro found
corner lots not relevant.

Mixed occupancy
It has already been stated that all studies of
burglary found that low occupancy was a major
factor in burglary risk. Reppetto found that
burglary rates were higher in areas with low
occupancy during the day and, in the Toronto
study, victimised houses were much less occupied during the day. Eighty per cent of the
victimised houses in the Kent study had been
unoccupied at the time of the burglary.

Waller and Okihiro suggest that the ideal
occupancy is a conventional family of two
parents and children with one parent working.
They also believe that such an occupancy is
likely to benefit neighbouring houses, as the
presence of people through the day and particularly children and around a house provides
ample opportunities for surveillance.

*'If we want to prevent burglary, we should be
trying to mix residences in which occupants are
largely absent within an area of houses with
children. Similarly, it may be functional for
prevention of crime (burglary) to retain distinct-
ly ethnic areas; where several generations
occupy the same household, the house is unlikely
to be vacant for long periods'.*

The following pattern is somewhat speculative, but it does seem reasonable to believe that
mixed developments of houses would more likely vary occupancy rates.

Pattern 4.10
Mixed development of houses

**In any housing layout or in-fill development,
vary the size and room composition of houses to
maximise the likelihood of a mixture of occupancies — families with children, retired people,
extended families, mixed with households composed entirely of working adults.**

Hardening of access points (windows and doors)
The recommendations for the protection of
apartments were mainly concerned with

'hardening' access points, rather than surveillance by others. The advantage of high- and medium-rise multi-unit structures is that there are few accessible entry points to individual dwellings compared with houses. For houses there are usually several doors and windows that are accessible and which offer potential entry points for burglary.

There seems to be general agreement among researchers that conventional ideas of improving locks on doors, adding chains and bolts and putting locks on openable windows have little value as crime prevention measures. Irvin Waller sums up his doubts about such measures under the title of 'security illusion':

'Interviews with residential burglars confirm the view that offenders who commit residential burglary more than once or twice are concerned about whether the residence is vacant or not. If it is vacant, and not easily visible by neighbours, it is difficult to prevent them entering. Even if the front door is solid, on a firm frame and locked with a dead bolt with a two-inch throw they can still try the back door, if not break a window. However, locks probably do deter the one-time young amateur, particularly if the residence is visible to neighbors or the street'. (Waller, 1979:9).

This Canadian point of view coincides precisely with the model already stated earlier in the chapter and is the same conclusion as drawn by the two more recent English studies by Maguire and by Jackson and Winchester. Waller in turn quotes from the earlier American study by ex-police officer Reppetto, who saw some value in improving the locks on apartment doors in the inner city where the unskilled burglars are most prominent but who believed that:

'Suburban home owners, however, who have many portals to secure against more highly skilled offenders would find this approach not cost-effective and would be better off simply purchasing insurance'. (Reppetto, 1974:85).

48

The data from the study by the Home Office research team illustrate very clearly how researchers have come to this conclusion. Winchester and Jackson (1982) found, as did other researchers, that the general level of security was low, but were able to classify houses into categories of 'good', 'partial' and 'poor' security. The definitions of these categories appear in *Table 4.4*. They compared their sample of victimised houses (from police records for the first nine months of 1979) with a random sample of houses from the same geographical area (general household sample).

It is clear from the table that only 12% of victimised houses had comprehensive security provision. The general household sample had even less security than the sample of those victimised which almost suggests that measures are counterproductive. However, it is easy to find explanations for victimised houses to have more security. Firstly, a number of victimised houses had been burgled more than once and the owners had responded by increased security measures. Furthermore, the study draws attention to the greater number of high value properties in the victim sample where owners not only knew that they had more to protect but would feel more able to pay for extra security devices to be installed.

Another reason why good security measures do not seem to be more effective than the conventional levels of security is that people often do not use the security measures they have. Twenty-two per cent of the residents in the general household sample admitted that they had left their house insecure on the last occasion on which they left the house unoccupied during the day. Even after being victimised, the Toronto study showed that residents were no more careful about locking up their houses than those who had not been victimised. This issue of 'carelessness' would become more important if consideration was given to crime prevention policies which make improved security mandatory on all householders.

TABLE 4.4 Security levels in victimised houses and a random sample of households *(Winchester and Jackson, 1982:20)*

Security level	Victim sample		General household sample	
Good security				
burglar alarm	20 (5%)		12 (3%)	
mortice deadlocks/doublelocks on all doors and window locks on all windows	10 (2%)	51 (12%)	7 (2%)	29 (6%)
mortice deadlocks/doublelocks on all doors and window locks on all downstairs windows	21 (5%)		10 (2%)	
Partial security				
some doors without mortice deadlocks/ doublelocks and/or some downstairs windows without window locks	269 (65%)		301 (66%)	
Poor security				
no mortice deadlocks or window locks	93 (23%)		128 (28%)	

A review of research into the current knowledge on crime and the built environment comments on a target-hardening project at Seattle that

'The study also presented evidence that the mode of entry of offenders changed after hardening. There was an increase in the percentage of entries through unlocked windows and doors'. (Rubenstein et al., 1980).

The same study appears to have been a more imaginative project than most studies based on fieldwork. It was the only study reviewers found which investigated 'pre-post' effects of hardening. The measures included not only dead-bolt locks and solid case doors but also the addition of short walls to prevent access (via windows, etc.) to interior door latches. The size of window opening was restricted to 9 in (230 mm), presumably to prevent physical access by male adults.

All the field studies which compare victims and non-victims included very few houses with more than basic security measures and it seems unlikely that such studies can really disprove the value of such measures. The plain fact is that in the cultural settings where these studies have been carried out there are only limited opportunities for selecting large samples of houses with well developed security provisions. For example, researchers would have to go to Spain and other European countries to sample modern houses with ornamental ironwork grills across all openable windows or with closeable external shutters (see, for example, *Figure 4.12*). Windows of modern apartments in Southern France left unoccupied for months at a time are now frequently protected by steel or aluminium roller shutters. Clearly, such security measures are far stronger than improved locks and may well be effective.

Within the research evidence available for this book, there are clues to suggest that a comprehensive approach might work. The Seattle study suggests limiting window openings. Maguire comments that some modern aluminium window systems discourage some of the burglars he interviewed. Newman and Franck used the idea of metal-framed louvre windows in their coding. There must be many ways of making access

Figure 4.12 Most research on burglary has been done in cultural settings where there are few houses with well-developed security provisions. We have to look to non-English-speaking cultures to find examples of modern housing in which more extensive security measures are part of the accepted design aesthetic. In this example of a house in Austria, all windows have some form of shutter or grill and the doors are very strongly contructed. (Photo by author)

more difficult without necessarily reducing the amenity of design. Locking systems for doors and windows need not be located adjacent to the dead-bolt; there are many new forms of glazing being introduced; safety glass or heavier thicknesses of glass would make breakage more difficult; and there is the introduction of methods of reinforcement with plastic films, etc. The only constraint is cost, which is the point already made by Thomas Reppetto.

In the absence of more detailed research into the effects of stronger security measures, the following principle is suggested in relation to the hardening of access points for any dwelling where the owner or occupier would like to reduce the risk of burglary.

Pattern 4.11
Securing windows and doors

Significantly improve the strength and access resistance of all accessible windows and doors uniformly. It would not suffice simply to add locks and similar devices; the use of stronger

materials and frames, grilles, etc. should be considered. There is little point in restricting measures to a proportion of access points.

It must be left to the owner or developer to decide the cost benefit. Where it is not considered to be an economic proposition to implement this pattern there is good sense in providing sound locks and bolts in the conventional manner, particularly in public housing, inner-city areas or any poor district of a town or city where amateur burglars are most likely to operate.

It is important to stress that whatever measures are taken over securing access points to houses, the more general patterns dealing with access and surveillance may still be the most effective. The combination of hardening, access control and surveillance may well prove to be a potent means of crime prevention. Well designed and protected houses would only be at risk from the most determined and experienced burglars, who would have a good idea about what they would find in the house.

5 Vandalism and public housing

One of the objectives of this book has been to bring together research findings from several countries, particularly from North America and Britain. However, this presents a particular difficulty with crime and public housing. It would be quite acceptable to criminologists on both sides of the Atlantic to claim that crime problems are associated with public housing. Baldwin and Bottoms (1976) reported in their studies of Sheffield that more offenders live on public housing estates than in owner-occupied housing. The impetus for Newman's ideas came from his experience of very high levels of crime on public housing projects in New York and elsewhere in the United States (Newman, 1972). A great deal of attention has been given to the problem of crime and fear of crime in American public housing, as for example in the United States Government's Interagency Urban Initiatives Anti-Crime Program (Department of Housing and Urban Development, 1980).

But the similarity stops at this point. The two situations of public housing in the United States and in Britain are very different. In Britain the public housing sector comprises more than 30% of all housing, but in the United States the proportion is much smaller, around 3%. Whereas, in Britain, the population living in council housing is in no way a socially under-privileged minority, those living in public housing in the United States would certainly be so regarded. The result of this difference seems to be that all American public housing is seen to present a crime problem, whereas in Britain there is only a minority of 'problem' or 'difficult' estates. American public housing is portrayed as having all kinds of crime: '. . . murder, assault, rape, robbery, burglary, larceny and auto theft rates

have risen dramatically over the last two decades in the United States; . . . and other forms of subsidised housing often have higher crime rates than many other neighbourhoods of larger cities; and fear of crime is widespread – especially in public housing' (Department of Housing and Urban Development, 1980).

In Britain the evidence for greatly increased crime rates in public housing is not available from formal statistics because these are not separated for different forms of tenure. However, the problem that has caught the attention of the public and given housing authorities much concern is vandalism; in particular, vandalism on the large housing estates in the inner areas of large cities, which were constructed of large blocks of flats and maisonettes. Research into the design aspects of crime prevention in public housing in Britain has, therefore, concentrated on the problem of vandalism. Because the differences between the American and British scenes are so considerable, this chapter is confined to research on vandalism in public housing in Britain.

Vandalism

Much of the research into vandalism in Britain has been initiated by the Home Office Research Unit (now known as the Home Office Research and Planning Unit). In trying to establish some general patterns on the occurrence of vandalism, Sturman attempted to assemble a record of all incidents of vandalism during a six-month period on a council estate in Manchester (Sturman, 1978). His data showed that public facilities seem more likely to be vandalised than the housing itself. His estimates, based mainly on victim surveys, give the rate of incidents for four main environmental categories during the six months as:

Incidents of damage per school	19.18
Incidents of damage per public telephone kiosk	7.81
Incidents of damage per shop	3.40
Incidents of damage per dwelling	0.04

He also points out that the risk of vandalism among dwellings is higher for flats and maisonettes than for the semi-detached houses which, therefore, appear to be the least vulnerable element on the estate.

The general impression is that incidents of damage are not as serious as popular treatment in the media suggests. Nevertheless, the study did show that criminal statistics do not record more than a small proportion of criminal damage. Sturman concluded that 'vandalism comprises a very large number of often trivial incidents . . . which only in aggregate become a serious problem'. The fact that damage tends to be to public facilities also draws the attention of public agencies who count the cost of many small incidents.

In support of this conclusion Gladstone found, from a study of self-reported vandalism among schoolboys, that vandalism was a common activity of their lives (Gladstone, 1978). He established very clearly that vandalism is not a crime committed by a delinquent minority. Analysis of questionnaires completed by 584 boys of between 11 and 15 years suggested that relatively minor vandalism, such as breaking a bottle in the street or a window in an empty house, was very widespread. More serious forms of vandalism, such as damaging phone-boxes, cars or bus seats, although less common were still quite frequent (see *Table 5.1*).

Defensible space and vandalism
Although Oscar Newman's book *Defensible Space* was concerned with all forms of criminal activity in housing projects, it contained many photographs of vandalism both outside and in the lobbies and other communal areas of high-rise housing blocks. Naturally this attracted the attention of architects, planners and housing managers in Britain who were faced with growing problems of vandalism in the large complex housing designs which had been built in Britain during the 1960s.

One of the Home Office Research Unit's projects attempted to explore to what extent

TABLE 5.1 **Percentage of boys admitting to have committed specific acts of vandalism in the previous six months** *(from Gladstone, 1978:23)*

The prevalence of vandalism

1	Scratched desk at school	85%
2	Broken a bottle in the street	79%
3	Broken a window in an empty house	68%
4	Written on walls in the street	65%
5	Broken trees or flowers in a park	58%
6	Written on the seats or walls of buses	55%
7	Broken the glass in a street lamp	48%
8	Scratched a car or lorry	42%
9	Smashed things on a building site	40%
10	Broken a window in an occupied house	32%
11	Broken the glass in a bus shelter	32%
12	Damaged park building	31%
13	Broken furniture at school	29%
14	Broken a window in a public toilet	29%
15	Broken the glass of a telephone kiosk	28%
16	Broken a car radio aerial	28%
18	Damaged the tyres of a car	28%
19	Broken a window at school	27%
20	Slashed bus seats	22%
21	Broken a seat in a public toilet	20%
21	Damaged telephone in a kiosk	20%
22	Put large objects on a railway line	19%
23	Broken a window in a club	16%
24	Slashed train seats	12%

defensible space ideas would be able to control the levels of vandalism in large-scale public housing in Britain. A study was made of vandalism on all estates of over 100 dwellings in two inner London boroughs (Wilson, 1978). The final research sample was based on 285 separate blocks of dwellings. More than half of these blocks had gallery or balcony access in either four- or five-storey blocks or slab blocks of nine storeys. Most of the other blocks were staircase access, towers with lifts and deck access blocks. There were a few terraces of row houses.

Figure 5.1 There was more vandalism in entrances which provided through routes to other blocks. (Photo by author)

A number of characteristics were assessed for each of these blocks which were considered to measure defensible space. These included height and size of blocks, the average number of dwellings sharing each entrance, and whether an entrance served only one block or also acted as a through route to other blocks. The spaces around the blocks were assessed as private, semi-private, semi-public or public after the hierarchy described by Newman. In assessing the amount of vandalism, local authority housing repair records were consulted and observations were also made of the apparent levels of vandalism on each block.

A number of other variables were also measured, most notably the number of children aged from 6 to 16 living in each block, which information was available from education wel-

fare records. It was found that the number of children per dwelling was an overriding factor in predicting levels of vandalism, far more important than the physical design variables. However, once some control for child density was added to the analysis, it was found that blocks with lower child densities showed variations in vandalism that related to design factors. For example, there was more vandalism in entrances which provided through routes to other blocks. Where entrances led to only one block and through real or symbolic barriers that implied resident-only access, levels of vandalism were lower. This particularly applied to lift damage. Of those blocks with an entrance acting as a through route, 76% had five or more calls for lift repairs, whereas for blocks with discrete entrances serving only one block only 30% had this number of call-outs.

Despite these small successes at establishing the value of defensible space, the author seems to have been disappointed that the study showed such a small effect. However, this is not altogether surprising. If the measures used to assess the degree of defensible space are examined more closely, they seem to represent Newman's model rather incompletely. Newman was concerned with creating semi-public and semi-private areas, between public streets and private dwellings, which could be observed from dwellings and so control their use. The Wilson study of London estates did not attempt to measure surveillance from dwellings. There seems little evidence from the study to suggest that the types of design included in the 285 blocks included semi-public or semi-private areas which could be observed from dwellings. In other words there seems to have been very little defensible space in the sample of housing studied.

However, the study does seem particularly valuable in that it has assembled a great deal of data on the distribution of vandalism. It appears to confirm that most damage occurred in these semi-public and semi-private areas which were

TABLE 5.2 Location of damage on Inner London housing estates *(from Wilson, 1978:54)*

	Lifts	Private dwellings	Stairs corridors walkways	Communal facilities*	Entrances	Outside areas	Underground garages†	Roofs	Total
Number of items of damage	1643	1475	1416	776	361	289	176	89	6225
Percentage	26	24	23	12	6	5	3	1	100

* 'Communal facilities' covers tenants' store-sheds, cupboards for fittings, caretaker's rooms, laundries etc.

† Several underground garages had, because of vandalism, ceased to be used and had been left unrepaired, so the figure given is likely to be an underestimate.

indefensible. It can be seen from *Table 5.2* that most of the damage occurred in the shared communal parts of the blocks. Only 24% occurred to dwellings and most of this was window breakage at the ground floor level. A significant minority of the dwellings were vandalised while empty. The lifts attracted most vandalism, with stairs, corridors and walkways the next most common locations. Other target areas included communal storage and laundries and underground garages. Such findings seem to be in perfect accord with Newman's analysis.

Perhaps a more searching research design which contained samples of blocks (like Newman's Brownsville Houses) which had good defensible space characteristics including surveillance from dwellings, and samples of blocks without such characteristics, may have shown that even with high child densities differences in levels of vandalism were significant. However, the findings from this study do show that semi-public and semi-private spaces in and around public housing are liable to vandalism if there is no supervision. If defensible space theory is to be *proved* then it will be necessary to find out if supervision or surveillance of these spaces is sufficient to discourage vandalism. So far no such evidence is available.

Bearing in mind Sturman's point that flats and maisonettes (various forms of apartment) had more vandalism than houses, and that Wilson's study shows that most vandalism was in com-

munal access areas, there seems to be a fundamental preference for housing forms which eliminate communal access spaces and have, therefore, direct access from public areas to private apartments. Newman's diagram showing a

Figure 5.2 Most vandalism in large housing blocks occurred in communal access areas, including lifts, stairs, corridors and walkways, particularly where there was extensive glazing. (Photo by author)

54

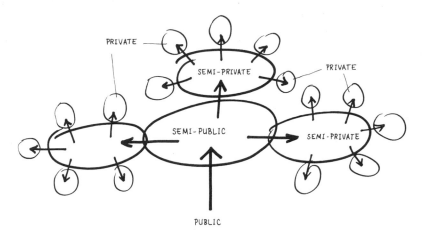

Figure 5.3 Newman's
defensible space hierarchy.
(From Newman, 1972).
(Courtesy Oscar Newman)

hierarchy of defensible space (similar to *Figure
5.3*) can be seen as a compromise solution to the
organisation of space in massive housing blocks.

The design of such multiple dwelling blocks
forces a breakdown in the traditional arrangement of direct access from public street to private dwelling (see *Figure 5.4*). Not only does the
traditional form eliminate the problem of semi-
public and semi-private areas, but it also provides natural surveillance of the street from the
dwellings (very much after the ideas of Jane
Jacobs, 1962).

As Wilson suggests in a more recent paper
(Wilson, 1981), Newman's theory is unnecessarily elaborate. If there is a need for housing
forms other than the traditional house-on-the-
street form (*Figure 5.4*) then the spaces in

Newman's hierarchy diagram labelled 'semi-
public' and 'semi-private' must be minimised
and access to them strictly controlled. Indeed,
this is what has been happening with the modification programmes to try to improve local
authority housing. Communal entrance areas
are being fitted with doors and these are controlled by various locking systems.

Already in Chapter 4 there has been some
discussion of the problems of creating controlled
access by burglary prevention in apartment
buildings. Mention was also made in that discussion of vandalism, which was as much of a
problem as burglary, so that pattern 4.2 is
almost certainly relevant here.

In summary it would seem that the following
pattern is the preferred pattern for housing
design:

Pattern 5.1
Preferred access form for dwellings

**Access to dwellings should be as direct as possi-
ble from public areas, without intermediate
semi-private and semi-public spaces.**

Where this preference cannot be exercised, particularly where an attempt is being made to
improve existing accommodation, the pattern
described in 4.2 is also applicable here.

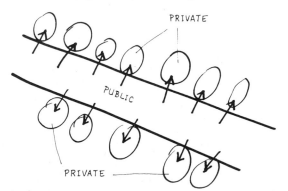

Figure 5.4 Traditional
pattern of direct access
from public street to private
dwelling

Some further support for the preference for pattern 5.1 comes from a project to modify four three-storey walk-up flat blocks in Liverpool which explicitly attempted to use Newman's ideas about defensible space (Hunter, 1978). The blocks had suffered from a good deal of vandalism. They were surrounded by a desert of asphalt paving. Strangers could walk up to the ground floor windows. Intruders could enter the stair halls and break into flats, and there were problems of vagrants using the stairwells and landings overnight. Windows and light fittings in the stair halls were permanently broken and outside had much graffiti and litter as the area was used by children and teenagers from adjacent housing estates.

Under the influence of Newman's ideas, Hunter and his associates planned a number of physical modifications after some consultation with the tenants. These included essentially three elements. The stairwells were to have doors fitted and an entry-phone system installed. The stairwells were also to be cleaned and painted. Outside, the grounds around the blocks were to be fenced with a substantial timber fence about 6 ft (1.8 m) high, to create private yards or gardens for ground-floor flats and to form two 'semi-private' spaces between blocks with restricted access to residents on upper floors. Planting and trees and shrubs were provided to soften the general appearance.

The result of these modifications is quite instructive. Only the private gardens and yards survived and indeed some of the newly created gardens were being well cared for. Although the fencing around private gardens was left undamaged, the fencing around the semi-private areas was broken down, presumably by local children and young people who wished to regain access to the area. The doors to the common stair halls were removed and the entry phone torn out of the wall. The fact that in this hard area 'private' areas were undamaged and the adjacent semi-private areas were destroyed suggests that pattern 5.1 is a very robust relationship.

Figure 5.5 Part of Railway Court in Sunderland before partial demolition. It was a four-storey masionette development with communal stairs and all grounds around the blocks were communal. The blocks were heavily vandalised and difficult to let. (Photo by courtesy of the Director of Architecture, Borough of Sunderland)

Figure 5.6 The top two storeys of Railway Court being demolished. (Photo by courtesy of the Director of Architecture, Borough of Sunderland)

Figure 5.7 The converted houses after demolition of upper storeys. Each house has its own front and back gardens. There is no semi-private or semi-public space, the private gardens are entered directly from the street; see pattern 5.1. (Photo by courtesy of the Director of Architecture, Borough of Sunderland)

Figure 5.8 An example, before conversion, of a three-storey housing block at North Kenton in Newcastle upon Tyne. Access to flats and maisonettes was via communal stairs and the grounds surrounding the block were communal. The block suffered serious vandalism and was difficult to let. (Photo by courtesy of Newcastle upon Tyne City Council, City Engineer's Dept)

Figure 5.9 The same block as in Figure 5.8 after conversion into three-storey town houses. Note that not only has communal access been eliminated but the space around the block has been used as private gardens and each house has its own integral garage. (Photo by courtesy of Newcastle upon Tyne City Council, City Engineer's Dept)

It is perhaps worth emphasising that what is proposed by the preferred pattern 5.1 is the elimination of housing forms which contain semi-private and semi-public spaces. It implies the elimination of multi-unit dwelling blocks with common entrance areas, shared stairs, lifts etc. This relates closely with pattern 3.3 already identified in Chapter 3 on safer neighbourhoods. The most obvious application of the pattern is in new house building.

There is little doubt that this pattern has been taken seriously by many local authorities who have abandoned high-rise forms of housing and the deck-access designs of the 1960s and are insisting on building only conventional houses. There is also evidence that local housing managements are making fundamental structural changes to existing public housing projects that have become 'difficult to let' for a variety of reasons.

It was reported by Chris Tighe (1981) that four-storey walk-up maisonette blocks in Sunderland built in the 1960s, with shared stair access, have been reduced to two-storey terraced houses by demolishing the top two floors (*Figures 5.5–5.7*). In this way the 'unpopular and much abused communal entrances and staircase cores were removed and absorbed into the new dwellings'. The houses now have individual front and rear entrances and private fenced-in gardens. Another scheme in nearby Newcastle included the conversion of three-storey blocks from a mixture of maisonettes and flats to terraces of three-storey 'town houses' (*Figures 5.8 and 5.9*). Both schemes are reported to be very popular among tenants.

Even where such fundamental changes to housing are not practicable or economic more limited modifications might be possible. *Figure 5.10* illustrates an example of a deck-access scheme in the same area which was studied by Sheena Wilson. Here the network of galleries, linked by bridges between blocks, was very extensive. Problems arose from vandalism and

Figure 5.10 A deck-access scheme on the Loughborough Estate in Lambeth in which most of the galleries serving the upper level of maisonettes were interconnected by bridges. However, this created an extensive network of walkways which encouraged children and youths to roam about the scheme which led to vandalism and other nuisance including more serious crimes. (Photo by author)

Figure 5.11 To reduce the problems caused by children and youths wandering through the upper galleries, access to bridges was fenced off, but even these barricades were soon broken down. (Photo by author)

other crimes and general nuisance caused by children and youths roaming these 'semi-public' areas. In an attempt to reduce the problem and limit accessibility of these galleries, the housing authority blocked off access to the bridge links (see *Figure 5.11*). This measure proved ineffective as the barriers were soon broken down. It was finally decided to demolish the bridge links (see *Figure 5.12*) although this was unacceptable to the fire authorities where the removal of the bridge links removed alternative escape routes from individual dwellings.

Child densities
From all the references to vandalism there is frequent mention of the presence of children. Sheena Wilson's principal finding, that child density was a more dominant factor in determining levels of vandalism than physical design, was

Figure 5.12 Workmen removing linking bridges in the hope of reducing vandalism and other crime or nuisance. Note also that the communal garages originally provided on the ground floors of these blocks are no longer used because of risk of theft and vandalism. (Photo by author)

also reflected in another English study of damage to 217 telephone kiosks in Greenwich (Mayhew *et al.,* 1979). The two most important factors emerging from this study were that kiosks were more likely to be heavily damaged in council housing areas and where the population of boys was highest. There does seem to be a good case from this evidence to consider controlling child densities in local authority housing.

Wilson pointed out that efforts were already being made to allocate new tenants to housing with this in mind. Also, where local authorities are rehabilitating older blocks, modifications can be made to change the size of units to achieve mixes of one-, two- and three-bedroom dwellings. No clear guideline can be given for recommending maximum child densities. The study by Wilson defined blocks with low child densities as containing an average of three or less children per ten dwellings, but this would be too stringent as a guideline for housing allocation policies. However, what might be a more realistic approach would be to limit allocation of new tenancies in blocks with large amounts of unsupervisable communal space to all-adult households. This can be defined as a pattern for housing management:

Pattern 5.2
Allocation and child density

If an apartment building has substantial unsupervised communal areas and lacks any means of access control (see pattern 4.2) units should be allocated to as many all-adult households as possible.

Tenant involvement and consultation
The recognition from research that social factors are usually more dominant than design form in determining levels of vandalism, raises the important question of housing management and tenant involvement in housing management. Even where a public housing estate comprises houses rather than multi-unit structures, prob-

lems of vandalism can arise. A well-researched case in point is the Cunningham Road estate in Widnes. This estate was chosen 'to test out the theory that only if people have a sense of belonging and responsibility for the place in which they live will they want to look after it and improve it' (Hedges, Blaber and Mostyn, 1980).

The estate consisted of 450 houses with front and rear gardens. It had a population of about 1600, of whom nearly half were aged under 17.

'. . . the older part of the estate was run down. Most of the gardens were untended; fencing was a jumble of corrugated iron, wire and old boarding . . . The streets were in poor condition, the pavements worse, and there were no trees in public places . . . There were signs of vandalism all over the old part of the estate: broken glass, graffiti on "undefended" walls, smashed brickwork, and litter strewn around gardens, pavements and streets.'

To set about tackling the estate, NACRO (National Association for the Care and Resettlement of Offenders) and SCPR (Social and Community Planning Research) began a process of consultation with residents of the estate, often in the form of invited small groups, to try to establish what they felt was needed to improve the condition of the estate. From this process a Residents Association was formed and gradually ideas were developed for improvement both in terms of practical measures and methods of communication with the various local authority departments responsible for the estate.

A great many issues were dealt with, including the painting of houses, better systems for dealing with repairs and maintenance, the provision of a beat policeman, play facilities, improvements and repairs to pavements, fencing to gardens, street lighting repairs, street cleaning and the planting of trees and shrubs. Implementation took place over a period of three years (1976–9) and, by the end of this period

'the appearance and atmosphere of the estate have improved enormously, and there are signs

that many tenants are responding by caring more for their gardens and their environment'. (Hedges, Blaber and Mostyn, 1980).

The monitoring team attempted to establish how far vandalism had been reduced. In general, residents felt that there was less damage to houses and shops as a result of the changes, although now that there was tree and shrub planting in some of the public areas, it was felt that vandalism had increased there. Unfortunately, the evidence on vandalism was based mainly on questionnaire surveys rather than repair records or other more objective measures. Nevertheless, two points emerge from this project which might be more generally applicable:

1 Quicker repair and maintenance. The evidence is not strong here but the results of a project like Cunningham Road are believed to demonstrate that by raising the quality of maintenance of the houses and by improving the response to requests for repair, less wilful damage will occur. It has to be admitted that it is hard to come by reliable statistical evidence; for example, when a quicker repair policy was adopted for street lighting the number of repairs increased at first, but this may have been the result of inadequate repairs previously. The idea of quicker repair has been advanced by Clarke (1978:72) who also admits that good evidence is scarce.

2 Reduction of target in public places. The discovery that vandalism increased when targets were introduced in public areas on the estate would not be surprising to anyone who has been responsible for tree-planting programmes on housing estates. As the monitoring report on the Cunningham Road project points out 'what does not exist cannot be damaged'.

There seems to be an important principle here which is an extention of the more conventional notion of target hardening. The most effective way to avoid vandalism in public areas is to eliminate targets that cannot stand up to damage. Unfortunately the question of target hardening has received little methodical research, but two references may be of interest. The first is an earlier Building Research Station Digest *Wilful Damage on Housing Estates* (Department of the Environment, 1971), and the second, a chapter in the book on vandalism edited by Colin Ward, called *What an architect can do: A series of design guides* (Leather and Matthews, 1973).

Although there is little research evidence the principles of target hardening and target elimination are so well established in practice that it seems worth presenting a general pattern statement here:

Pattern 5.3
Public areas in housing schemes

Objects and surfaces in public areas of housing schemes (particularly in public housing) should be either 'hardened' to reduce risk of damage, or removed.

Two further comments should be made on the Cunningham Road project. Although the monitoring team admit the difficulty of their task in measuring changes in a complex setting, two factors should be noted when judging the results of the project. The external setting of the estate appears to have been changing considerably. It was described as 'set in the middle of what was, until 1973, a vast scrap and rubbish dump', but it is 'now reclaimed, landscaped and made into a nine-hole golf course'. Secondly, there seems to have been a drop in the number of children on the estate during the monitoring period, particularly in what was the worst part of the estate. Knowing the findings already mentioned here on child density, we have to be cautious about the interpretation of results.

It will be interesting to see the results of future projects by NACRO, both their Safe Neighbourhoods Unit and the Crime Prevention Unit which are extending the ideas of tenant consultation to the improvement of a number of public housing estates in London and elsewhere in the country. Similar ideas of tenant consultation and involvement are being followed, with less emphasis on crime prevention, in the Priority Estates Projects of the Department of the Environment, which are attempting to improve badly run-down public housing estates.

6 Street attacks in city centres

Mention has already been made in Chapter 3 of robbery which involves violent interaction between an offender and the victim. This chapter presents some of the findings from a study of all crimes where individuals had been attacked or assaulted in public places, including thefts such as pickpocketing. The study was carried out in the city centres of Birmingham and Coventry and based on observations of activity in these cities and data from police crime files for the year September 1977 to August 1978 (Poyner, 1980). The study suggested a number of patterns for the design and management of city centres. Although they apply specifically to these two cities, they may well apply equally to other British cities and in a more analogous way elsewhere.

Crimes included were: violent and sexual assaults, robbery and theft from the person. The main focus of the study was the 552 attacks reported in the central area of Birmingham, but the study also looked at a sample of one month in three of attacks reported in the city centre of Coventry and the surrounding suburbs. Only those attacks which occurred in public places were included – that is streets, pedestrian areas, car parks, open spaces and waste ground. Assaults and robberies in shops, offices and dwellings were excluded. Assaults on the police and security personnel are also excluded from the data presented here.

Classification of street attacks

As shown in previous chapters, police crime categories often contain a wide variety of behaviour, which makes it difficult to give precise recommendations for prevention. This is parti-

cularly true of the wide range of behaviour included in the police categories in this study. For example, the category of 'wounding' can include an argument between husband and wife that became violent, bullying by schoolboys, or a fight outside a pub after closing time. Similarly, the category of 'robbery' can include a gang raid on a security van in which firearms were used or a case of older children taking a small sum of money from younger children. Categories such as 'theft from the person' or 'sexual assault' are equally diverse.

In order to work out appropriate forms of prevention for such a diverse range of behaviour, it is necessary to separate the different types of criminal behaviour. To achieve this, each crime was analysed in terms of the processs model shown in *Figure 6.1*. The model represents a

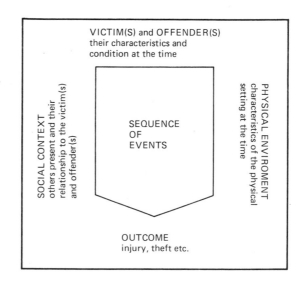

Figure 6.1 A process model for street attacks

crime as the *outcome* of a *sequence of events* which involve the *victim and offender*. As far as possible it is seen as important to record the characteristics of the victim and offender as well as the *social context* and the *physical environment* or setting. The data were drawn from the police crime files, from visits to the scenes of crimes, and from more general observation of activity and use of the areas in which crime occurred.

The best way to illustrate the use of the model is to give an example. *Figure 6.2* summarises what was known about an incident in which a man was attacked while walking home. By setting down the sequence of events which led up to the incident, it is much easier to understand the nature of the attack and how the various factors came together. The victim was very much the worse for drink when the offender first found him. It is quite likely that the offender had no

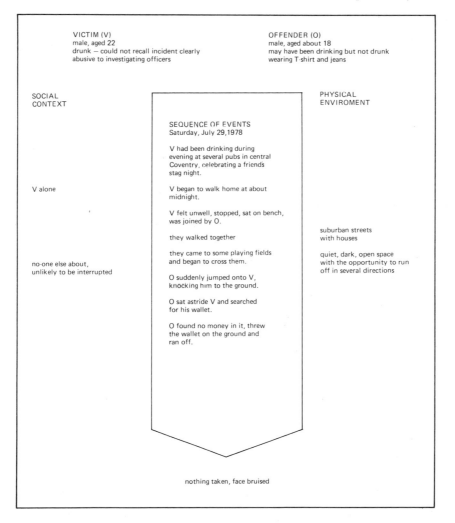

VICTIM (V)
male, aged 22
drunk — could not recall incident clearly
abusive to investigating officers

OFFENDER (O)
male, aged about 18
may have been drinking but not drunk
wearing T-shirt and jeans

SOCIAL CONTEXT

PHYSICAL ENVIROMENT

SEQUENCE OF EVENTS
Saturday, July 29, 1978

V had been drinking during evening at several pubs in central Coventry, celebrating a friends stag night.

V began to walk home at about midnight.

V alone

V felt unwell, stopped, sat on bench, was joined by O.

they walked together

suburban streets with houses

they came to some playing fields and began to cross them.

no-one else about, unlikely to be interrupted

quiet, dark, open space with the opportunity to run off in several directions

O suddenly jumped onto V, knocking him to the ground.

O sat astride V and searched for his wallet.

O found no money in it, threw the wallet on the ground and ran off.

nothing taken, face bruised

Figure 6.2 An example of the process model in use

TABLE 6.1 A comparison of the numbers of street attacks occurring in the city centre of Birmingham and in central and suburban Coventry from September 1977 to August 1978

	Birmingham city centre	Coventry city centre	Coventry suburbs
VIOLENT ASSAULTS			
Fights and brawls after drinking	56	39	60
Attacks made by football supporters	18	—	6
Assaults on children	3	3	69
Conflict from a sexual relationship	15	—	6
Other disputes between known persons	4	3	33
Other assaults by strangers	22	9	42
Too little information to classify	19	3	18
	137	57	234
ATTACKS FOR GAIN			
Robbery from a kiosk	5	—	—
Robbery of drunks	7	12	33
Other robbery of people in the street	24	9	12
Money snatches while being taken to the bank	9	3	—
Handbag snatches	31	—	45
Purses/money snatches from the hand	20	—	6
Pickpocketing while boarding a bus	30	3	3
Other pickpocketing	38	—	—
Thefts from shopping bags	205	3	—
Theft and robbery from children	11	—	15
Other attacks for gain	5	—	—
Too little information to classify	10	6	6
	395	36	120
SEXUAL ASSAULTS			
Quick grabs	13	15	12
Attempted rape	1	—	18
Interfering with children	—	—	18
Other sexual assaults	6	—	33
	20	15	81
Total street attacks on the public	552	108	435

intention to rob the victim, but it was perhaps only when he found himself in a dark, open and unobserved place that the opportunity for robbery occurred to him. The fact that he found no money is quite consistent with earlier events. The victim probably spent all his money celebrating his friend's stag night, and it was because he had no money that he was walking home.

When a large number of crimes have been represented in this form, it is interesting to see that some are very similar – almost identical. It is possible to group these similar cases together and build up a much more detailed and useful classification of crimes for the purpose of considering crime prevention. Once clear patterns can be shown to exist in the events which lead to crimes, it is comparatively easy to identify possible ways of intervening to prevent crime.

The classification of crimes which emerged from this study is given in *Table 6.1*. It is divided into three main sections: violent assaults, attacks for gain and sexual assaults. The data are shown separately for the two city centres and the suburban area of Coventry, and indicate the number of assaults reported in a year. The number of reports for Coventry was multiplied by three to give an equivalent set of annual figures.

Before discussing the implications for crime prevention of these categories of assault, it is worth noting the differences in the pattern of crime found in the three areas. Although the geographical area of the two city centres is very similar (central Coventry is 0.95 km^2 and central Birmingham 0.89 km^2) the amount of crime is very different. Birmingham centre has more than five times the crime of Coventry's city centre. This is almost certainly due to the intensity of use of the two centres.

Birmingham is Britain's second city with just over a million inhabitants and it is the centre of a large conurbation. Coventry has a population of about a third of a million. Compared with the city centre of Coventry, its suburban area has four times the crime, but it is almost exactly 100

times the area (96 km^2). This shows very clearly that the types of crime under consideration in this chapter are very much associated with city centres. In the suburbs the pattern of violence is less likely to be in public places and is more concerned with family conflict.

Comparison of the specific groups of crime also shows marked differences in distribution. For example, pickpocketing, thefts from shopping bags and purse snatches are almost entirely confined to the centre of Birmingham. Offences against children, both violence and sexual assault, tend to be suburban crimes. Indeed most sexual assaults tended to be in the suburban area with the exception of 'quick grabs' which were more characteristic of city-centre crime. The robbery of drunks was more characteristic of Coventry, particularly the suburbs. As might be expected, disputes between people known to each other was more common in suburban areas. Some of these crimes will be discussed in more detail, but it is easy to see that the different physical environments present different kinds of opportunity for crime, which in itself is evidence to support the idea that changes in the physical environment might prevent opportunities for crime to occur.

Some support for this classification of crimes against the person comes from a more recent study by Malcolm Ramsay of crime in the city centre of Southampton (Ramsay, 1982). His study was concerned with all types of reported crime but his classification of violence and theft is very similar to the one in this study. Although he finds the same categories of crime in the city centre the relative proportions are again different from those in Birmingham and Coventry. This appears to support the theory that opportunity for crime varies according to the extent and distribution of the various facilities in the city centre. The findings reinforce the notion that each city has its own unique crime profile which requires its own specific programme of preventive measures.

Scope for prevention

The underlying assumption of this book is that crime prevention is best tackled in terms of situational factors, and that social measures of crime prevention are not particularly effective when particular types of crime are considered in detail. This is not to say that social factors are not relevant. There can be little doubt that the crime problems presented by the classification in *Table 6.1* are substantially the product of social problems. Where information was available about the offenders it was found that they were predominantly young males from lower socio-economic groups, often with disturbed or unstable family backgrounds. Even when the offender was older, he was still of low socio-economic status and perhaps a social isolate with drink or sexual problems.

However, to attempt social remedies to crime through improvements in upbringing, education,

Figure 6.3 Pickpocketing while boarding a bus

employment opportunities, better housing or care services is a long-term matter. (Indeed, it seems rather arrogant and beyond the scope of crime prevention to aim at fundamentally changing society.) The situational approach to crime prevention, as it applies here, recognises that we are continually faced with the problem of managing our city centres as they develop and change. Given the society we have *now*, and the people who use the city centre *now*, what can be done to reduce crime both immediately and progressively over the next few years?

The best way of illustrating how detailed study of particular crimes can yield situational factors for prevention is by taking an example of one group of crimes from the classification. 'Pickpocketing while boarding a bus' is a very clearly defined group of thefts that took place mainly in central Birmingham. The thirty cases reported in the year were similar in many ways and can be summarised in the same way as individual cases in *Figure 6.2*. The summary for this group is given in *Figure 6.3*. All incidents involved groups of youths running up to buses as they were being boarded and jostling the head of the queue under some pretext of asking the driver where the bus was going. While they were pushing and shoving the queue one of them would remove a wallet from the back trouser pocket of their victim. In all cases the victims were late-middle-aged or elderly men.

Some elements in the definition of this group may seem unnecessarily detailed, but closer examination reveals that the facts set out in the diagram in *Figure 6.3* are all *necessary* to the crime. The victims are older men because it was this age group who tend to wear looser-fitting trousers and keep wallets or purses in the back pocket. The pay-as-you-enter bus provides a long slow-moving queue at rush hour, and as intending passengers approach the entrance to the bus they get out their money or bus passes

Figure 6.4 Long queues waiting to board buses in the centre of Birmingham at stops which had suffered from pickpocketing. It is easy to see how the offenders could watch for suitable victims as they searched for money or bus passes before entering the bus. (Photo by author)

(see *Figure 6.4*). It is easy for would-be offenders to observe potential victims to see where they put their wallets or purses. The location of the bus stops on busy shopping streets with wide pavements and projecting canopies not only provides a non-suspicious place to loiter and watch the bus queue but also obviates the need for specially constructed bus shelters. Bus shelters would have obscured the view of the queue and made the crime more difficult to plan.

Once a clear statement can be made of what is necessary to a crime, it is relatively easy to begin to see what changes could be made to prevent or at least reduce the risk of these crimes recurring. Typically, the types of situational intervention which emerge can be grouped under three headings: supervision and policing, environmental changes, and change in victim behaviour. For this example the following interventions seem appropriate:

1 *Supervision and policing.* The risk of these pickpocketing attacks on bus queues might be reduced if the head of the queue was supervised during the rush period by inspectors of the transport authority or by the police.

2 *Environmental change.* There are several ways in which environmental changes might disrupt the opportunity for pickpocketing the queues. Barriers or railings enclosing the queue would make queue jumping almost impossible. The provision of opaque screens would make it difficult for the would-be offenders to observe potential victims. Removing the bus stops from bus shopping areas might discourage the youths loitering near bus stops. Abandoning pay-as-you-enter buses would probably eliminate this kind of pickpocketing attack.

3 *Victim behaviour change.* Since all victims kept their wallets or purses in their back trouser pocket, there is every reason to believe that if no bus passenger used a back trouser pocket to keep his money the problem would be solved. He might either keep his money elsewhere or hold on to his wallet or purse until safely seated on the bus.

Of course, these are theoretical ideas for intervention; not only might they not work in practice, but they may be impractical for economic reasons or because there are other overriding factors to be taken into account. The abandoning of pay-as-you-enter buses, for example, might be a good crime-prevention idea, but it has obvious economic and operational implications for the transport authority which may well rule it out.

Policing and other forms of supervision are clearly practical in city centres, where there are large numbers of people and where the need for supervision is well established. Increasingly, other sources of security personnel are being provided to supervise shopping malls and car parking, and there are other people employed who can contribute to the general supervision such as shop keepers, doormen and the bus inspectors already mentioned in the example.

Similarly, the environment is continually being changed. Although many cities have been largely re-built since 1945, there are always some modifications and additions being made. Even if these are not specifically made for crime-prevention purposes, they may well have implications for crime and can be incorporated into a broader crime-prevention programme.

The third area of intervention – victim-behaviour change – presents more of a problem. It is true that many forms of robbery and theft can be thwarted by victims. As in the pickpocketing example above, victims of theft can be more careful about where they keep wallets and purses. There was evidence to suggest that when victims of handbag or purse snatches resisted the snatch, the offenders just ran away. The evidence from this study also suggested that victims of sexual assault (in city streets) stand little risk of actual rape or injury if they resist their attacker.

However, the idea of intervention in most situations by changing the victim's behaviour is academic rather than practical. The problem is how to make people behave in a less vulnerable way. As has been pointed out in Chapter 2, publicity does not seem effective in changing the behaviour of drivers in securing their cars (Riley and Mayhew, 1980). There is no reason to doubt that the same is true for street attacks. For example, in thefts of purses from shoppers (more of this later) the shopper is heavily pre-occupied with hunting for bargains on a market stall, there is a queue, it is crowded and noisy, and there is a sense of urgency to attract the stallkeeper's attention. Crime prevention is the last thing that the shopper will be thinking about; the demands of the environment are overriding. Similarly, a man under the influence of heavy drinking will be in no state to remember some publicity about modifying his behaviour; indeed, if his lifestyle is socially detached from a stable home setting, television and the other media are less likely to reach him.

It is with these arguments in mind that the study concluded that the two main approaches to prevention of street attacks in city centres are through policing and other supervision and through environmental design and modification. The examination of all the categories of crime in the classification presented in *Table 6.1* suggested a simplified way of classifying preventive measures. If groups of crimes occurred in a specific environmental pattern, that is, only in certain places or certain types of place, then it was likely that some form of environmental change would prevent or reduce crime. If, in addition to some specific environmental pattern, there was a tendency for the crimes to occur at certain times of the day or on certain days of the

week, it seemed possible that policing or some other supervision might effectively prevent crime. For example the policing of football crowds to reduce the risk of violence and vandalism is realistic because the problem occurs on specific days at specific times and in specific places.

The classification of preventive measures can be set out in a simple matrix as shown in *Figure 6.5*. Crime categories can be either 'time specific' or 'time not specific' and they can be either 'location specific' or 'location not specific'. If the crime is 'location specific' then it is probable that, at least in theory, there is an environmental crime prevention measure. If the crime is both 'location specific' and 'time specific' then there is a good possibility that policing or other supervision is possible. The figure shows the possibility of policing being considered even though a crime type is not locationally specific. This might be where it is known that troublesome crowds are likely to be in the city centre after a football game, but where the exact location of trouble cannot be planned.

It is possible to allocate the crime categories in the classification in *Table 6.1* to the four cells of the matrix in *Figure 6.5*. The result of such analysis is shown in *Figure 6.6*. If the pattern of a crime category was roughly predictable in terms of location or time, then it is classified under 'location specific' and/or 'time specific'. Where a crime category did not have any time or location pattern, or if there were too few cases to identify patterns, then it is allocated to the cell 'not specific to either time or location'.

The number of incidents listed in each cell of *Figure 6.6* is based on the data from the city centre of Birmingham. The analysis is very encouraging. It suggests that almost 70% (60+9) of the attacks could be prevented by various forms of design and management of the environment. Sixty per cent of the incidents could involve prevention through a combination of environmental change and policing. Only a quarter (25%) of the attacks were too random

	location specific	location not specific
time specific	supervision and policing environmental change	(supervision and policing)
time not specific	environmental change	

Figure 6.5 Opportunities for intervention in crime groups

	LOCATION SPECIFIC		LOCATION NOT SPECIFIC	
TIME SPECIFIC	Fights and brawls after drinking	56	Attacks made by football supporters	18
	Pickpocketing while boarding bus	30	Money snatched while being taken to	
	Other pickpocketing	38	the bank	9
	Thefts from shopping bags	205	Robbery of drunks	7
		329		34
		60%		6%
TIME NOT SPECIFIC	Robbery from a kiosk	5	Assaults on children	3
	Handbag snatches	31	Conflict from a sexual relationship	15
	Quick grabs	13	Other disputes between known	
		49	persons	4
		9%	Other assaults by strangers	22
			Other robbery of people in the street	24
			Purses/money snatched from the hand	20
			Theft and robbery among children	11
			Other attacks for gain	5
			Other sexual assaults	7
			Too little information to classify	29
				140
				25%

Figure 6.6 Types of street attack grouped by opportunity for intervention

(not specific to time or location) to be brought methodically into a crime-prevention programme.

Closer examination of the crimes which are locationally specific indicated four main groups of crime where changes in the design and management of the environment could lead to the reduction of crime. The four groups are:
— thefts in markets and covered shopping malls;
— violence after drinking;
— pickpocketing at bus stops;
— crime in pedestrian subways.

It must be emphasised that this analysis applied specifically to the centre of Birmingham. For the centre of Coventry, only the second and fourth of these groups applied. However, the general conclusion from this work seems to be that a significant amount of crime against individuals in public places, particularly city centres, can be prevented through design and management of the environment. These four crime groups are now discussed in detail.

Thefts in markets and covered shopping malls
This group of crimes involved the theft of purses or money from shopping bags. The victims were almost all women; purses were taken from the bags they were carrying while they were shopping in the city centre. The conditions were sufficiently crowded for the victim to have been jostled in the crowd without realising that someone had reached into her bag. In some cases the purses had been taken from the top of an open bag, some had been taken from side pockets and in some cases bags had been unzipped before the purse was taken. Little was known about the offenders as few were caught, but those who were caught worked alone, sometimes following their victim for a while waiting for the best opportunity to take the purse.

This type of theft formed the largest group in the classification in *Table 6.1*; 205 incidents were reported in central Birmingham in the period of the study. The problem may be much more serious than these data suggest, as it is almost certain that this type of crime is under-reported. Victims were not always clear where the theft had occurred; some believed that they had dropped their purse or left it somewhere, and even if they felt sure that the purse had been stolen they may have thought that the loss was too trivial to report. Furthermore, because the offenders are almost impossible to trace, unless they are caught red-handed, these crimes tend to receive little police attention.

What makes this group of crimes particularly interesting is the offences occur in very specific locations, which suggests that they may be preventable in terms of situational measures. Firstly, they are a phenomenon associated only with the Birmingham data (see *Table 6.1*). Secondly, within the city centre of Birmingham there were quite specific concentrations of these thefts around the Bull Ring area, as shown on the map in *Figure 6.7*. When classified by types of location, as in *Table 6.2*, it is clear that these thefts

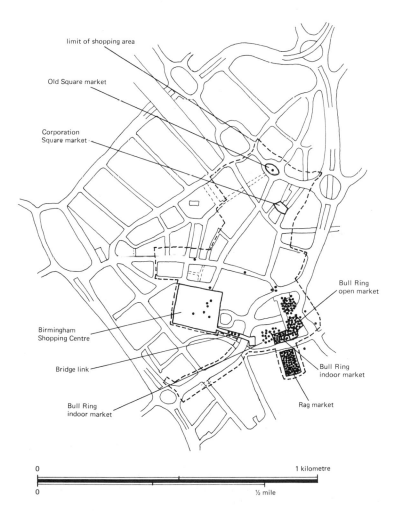

Figure 6.7 Distribution of thefts from shopping bags in Birmingham City Centre

TABLE 6.2 Location of thefts from shopping bags in Birmingham City Centre

Markets	158
Covered shopping malls	26
Subway systems	4
Shopping streets with traffic	3
Bus stops	2
Other	6
Unknown	6
Total	**205**

Figure 6.8 Thefts from shopping bags occur almost exclusively in the market areas of the city centre of Birmingham. Note the open-top shopping bags in use. (Photo by author)

occur almost exclusively in the markets (see *Figures* 6.8 and 6.9) with some in the covered shopping areas. The study excluded crimes inside shops and stores. However, it is known that the definition excluded a further twenty-seven thefts from shopping bags inside shops and stores, which only reinforces the importance of the market location for this type of crime.

As indicated in the matrix in *Figure 6.6*, this group of thefts is both time-specific and location-specific and therefore likely to be controlled by some form of policing or supervision. *Figure 6.10* shows a time chart of all the hours through the week with each incident plotted according to the hour of the day and the day of the week it occurred. The resulting distribution shows how strongly patterned in time is this type of theft. It occurs when the markets are at their busiest. The peak periods occur on Tuesday, Friday and Saturday. On Tuesday the peak period is during lunchtime, but on Friday and Saturday the peak is early afternoon after lunch. Saturday is by far the busiest day for these markets and this is clearly reflected in the data.

It is interesting to see that policing might be quite effective if it was concentrated on the peak periods of the week. However, it is even more interesting to look at the data in greater detail.

Table 6.3 shows how these thefts are distributed through the days of the week in the various locations. It can be seen from this table that the peak location is the Rag Market on Tuesdays. In fact the market is open only three

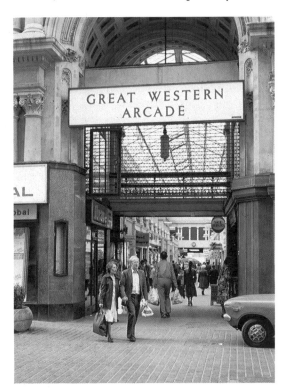

Figure 6.9 It is interesting to note that other shopping environments do not suffer from thefts from bags. This shopping arcade in Birmingham had no such theft reported. The essential conditions for the theft are not present even though people are equally laden with shopping bags. (Photo by author)

days a week (Tuesday, Friday and Saturday) and this appears to contribute to the pattern of peaks on these three days. The next most effective policing might be in the Open Market and Rag Market on Saturday, with perhaps only the Open Market being policed on Friday. By limiting policing to these peak times and locations, it is reasonable to believe that there could be a deterrent effect that would discourage offenders seeking opportunities to thieve in these markets.

If the pattern of crime through the year is analysed, as in *Table 6.4*, it may be feasible to police during the four peak months of May–August only.

The study does not suggest that policing will be an effective measure for crime prevention, but it does show that with careful analysis of the pattern of incidents, relatively modest man-power could be used to experiment with various forms of patrolling. Not only do the data show

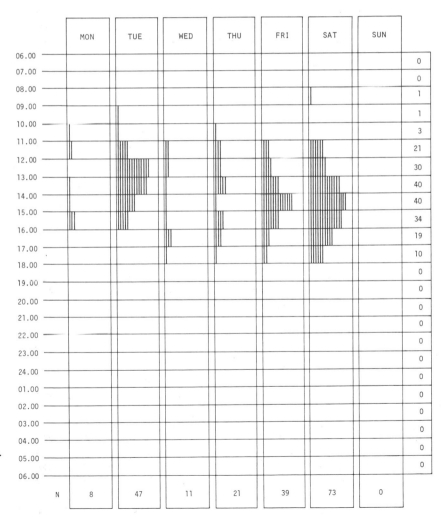

Figure 6.10 Time chart for thefts from shopping bags in Birmingham City Centre. The total of 205 incidents included 6 incidents for which information was insufficient to plot

TABLE 6.3 Distribution of thefts from shopping bags by day of the week in Birmingham City Centre

	Mon.	Tues.	Wed.	Thurs.	Fri.	Sat.	Sun.	Not known	Totals
Bull Ring Open Market	2	10	4	10	17	24	–	2	69
Rag Market*	–	31	–	–	11	21	–	–	63
Bull Ring Indoor Market**	2	3	2	2	4	11	–	1	25
Bull Ring Shopping Centre	3	–	2	1	4	6	–	–	16
Birmingham Shopping Centre	–	–	–	2	1	2	–	1	6
Bridge link	–	–	–	1	1	2	–	–	4
Other	1	2	3	3	1	6	–	–	16
Location not known	–	1	–	2	–	2	–	1	6
Totals	8	47	11	21	39	74	–	5	205

* Open only on Tuesdays, Fridays and Saturdays.
** Closed on Wednesday afternoon.

TABLE 6.4 Distribution of thefts from shopping bags by month

	J	F	M	A	M	J	J	A	S	O	N	D	Not known	Totals
Bull Ring Open Market	–	3	1	4	11	20	10	8	5	1	2	2	2	69
Rag Market	1	2	–	8	16	12	8	8	2	–	5	1	–	63
Bull Ring Indoor Market	–	2	2	4	4	2	2	6	1	–	–	2	–	25
Bull Ring Shopping Centre	–	2	–	2	1	1	1	1	1	3	1	3	–	16
Birmingham Shopping Centre	2	–	–	3	–	–	1	–	–	–	–	–	–	6
Bridge link	1	–	–	–	–	–	–	–	–	1	–	2	–	4
Other	2	1	3	–	–	–	2	–	2	–	2	4	–	16
Location not known	–	2	–	–	–	–	–	2	1	1	–	–	–	6
Totals	6	12	6	21	32	35	24	25	12	6	10	14	2	205

where and when policing is most likely to be effective, but they would also allow similar data to be collected to evaluate any policing experiment that is attempted.

It is often argued that displacement of crime to other areas undermines the effectiveness of measures, particularly when they are concentrated on one particular location. The advantage of data in the form discussed above is that any displacement effect of an experiment could be fully monitored. However, it seems unlikely that thefts from shopping bags would be significantly displaced beyond market areas because the environment in no way offers the same opportun-

ity. Indeed, it might be found that effective policing of market areas removed the attractiveness for prospective offenders to come to Birmingham and so reduce the level of these thefts elsewhere in the city centre.

Design and planning measures
It is worth emphasising some important aspects of the physical distribution of these thefts. First, the problem is largely confined to the main complex of retail markets around the Bull Ring area of Birmingham. There were also three other markets in the area studied, two small markets in central Birmingham (shown in *Figure 6.7*) and

one in Coventry. There were virtually no thefts of this kind reported in these three markets. It is true that the two other Birmingham markets are small, and one is only open once a week, but the Coventry Market is not much smaller than the Bull Ring Open Market and both are open most of the week.

Clearly the complex of markets around the Bull Ring is seen by would-be thieves as providing the 'best' opportunity for this kind of crime. It is a major facility drawing customers from all over the West Midlands helped by its central position near to transport (central rail and bus stations) and, because of its extent and the large crowds, it is logical to assume that people deliberately come to this area to thieve.

It seems likely that any planning policy which allows such a massive concentration of markets must be partly responsible for the higher level of this type of crime. One approach which might reduce the probability of this kind of theft becoming so prevalent would be to reduce the concentration of markets by dispersing the market areas among other elements of the city centre.

Although commercial and customer interests in the convenience of having one large complex may outweigh crime-prevention considerations, it is a measure that should, perhaps, be given greater weight in the planning of future market complexes. It is easy to understand why the Bull Ring complex was developed from traditional market locations and the rationalisation of public transport facilities during the post-war redevelopment of the city, but there are other cities which have several separate market locations. The pattern suggested by this evidence which might reduce the risk of theft in market areas is:

Pattern 6.1
Dispersion of market facilities

Retail market areas in cities should be dispersed to several locations rather than grouped into single large complexes.

The second environmental factor which appears to increase the opportunity for thefts from shopping bags is the layout of the market stalls. The 'totals' columns of *Tables 6.3* and *6.4* show the number of these thefts in the three markets of the Bull Ring complex. Comparison of the figures for the Indoor and Open Bull Ring Markets shows that the Indoor Market had far fewer of these thefts and yet the Indoor Market is larger in terms of both area and number of stalls. The two markets are immediately adjacent and open on the same days of the week. The Indoor Market also had fewer thefts from shopping bags than the Rag Market, even though the Rag Market was open only three days a week. Both the Rag Market and the Indoor Markets are under cover and similar in size.

The Indoor Market differs from the other two markets in that it is provided with permanent stalls built with wide access ways between each bank of stalls (minimum width of about 3 metres). The most crowded parts of the Rag Market and the Open Market have portable stalls set up with narrow gangways which are only 2 metres wide in many places (see *Figure 6.11*).

The importance of this difference becomes obvious when it is considered how the thefts from shopping bags take place. In the narrow gangways, shown in diagram A of *Figure 6.12*, when customers are lining the stalls on both sides of the gangway, the space left for people to walk between the stalls is so limited that everyone has to brush past each other (made even worse with pushchairs, etc.) Under these conditions it is relatively easy for someone to take a purse out of a bag held by a customer queueing at a stall. The customers at the stalls will be preoccupied with their searching and trying to attract the attention of the stallholders. Typically, they hold their shopping bags at their side away from the stall, sticking out into the stream of people in the gangways, and well out of their visual field.

Where the access ways are wider in the Indoor Market, there is still dense queueing along the stalls or counters, but there is more space for people to move between the stalls, as in diagram B in *Figure 6.12*. This extra space avoids jostling, except under extreme conditions of crowding, which appears to eliminate the conditions under which these thefts flourish. It may also be that the greater the space around individuals the more likely other people in the crowd would see a thief at work, and this may deter such crime.

From this it seems reasonable to assume that thefts from shopping bags would be reduced in markets, or in any congested retail setting, if the following pattern is adopted:

Pattern 6.2
Gangway width in congested markets

Gangways between stalls or counters in congested market areas should be at least 3 metres wide.

Taking these two patterns together, they suggest alternative approaches to the planning of market areas in large cities. If there is a need to disperse market areas and to alleviate crowding around stalls, one approach might be to pedestrianise wide streets and use them, at least in part, for market stalls as shown in the drawing in *Figure 6.13*. As can be seen from these drawings, the streets would have to be spacious. Some traditional street markets, especially in cities like London, are associated with narrow crowded

Figure 6.11 Stalls in the crowded part of the Bull Ring Open Market in Birmingham. It is easy to see that the gangways are narrow enough to facilitate thefts from shopping bags. In this case the woman nearest the camera is holding her purse in her hand – which may be safer than putting it in her shopping bag. (Photo by author)

pavements, and, as might be expected from these findings, suffer from the same crimes as the Birmingham markets.

No doubt there would be many objections to this approach to market planning from public authorities and from existing businesses in the streets. Litter problems common to markets might spread to these market streets. These issues would have to be carefully considered in relation to local circumstances.

2.0 m

A

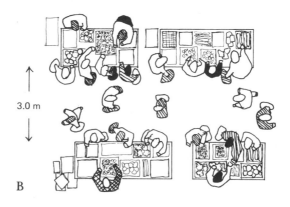

3.0 m

B

Figure 6.12 Effects of different gangway widths in markets

76

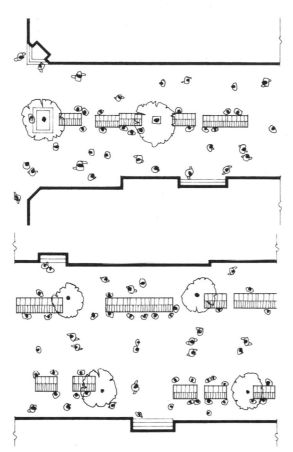

Figure 6.13 Examples of pedestrianised streets with market stalls

Violence after drinking

Fights and brawls after drinking formed the most important group of violent assaults in this study in both city centres. All these fights and brawls were between men who had been drinking at several places in the city centres during the evening. One or two of the victims may not have been drinking heavily, but all the offenders had. Some of the fights followed an earlier incident in a pub or drinking club. Others involved rowdy groups of drunken youths roaming the streets on their way home. These groups often comment to people passing or shout abuse at other groups or even try to provoke people by accusing them of staring: 'What are you staring at?', 'Are you looking for trouble?'. All the offenders were under thirty years old, and the victims were generally of the same age, though some were older. The victims were all strangers to the offenders.

Aggression appears to come easily in this state. Many of the offenders gave the impression that they were on the lookout for trouble and picked on people in order to provoke violence. In other situations quite trivial events led to arguments and violence. Offensive behaviour to women, odd forms of dress, just being stared at, or being from a racial minority, can provoke violence. Very often the victims behaved unwisely or seemed equally bent on violence. The violence was spontaneous; there was little warning.

These attacks are specific in time and location, because they all relate to drinking in the evening and most involve young men who use public transport to travel from the city centre to home. The time chart distribution is very clear in *Figure 6.14*. The heaviest problems are Friday and Saturday nights, but the patterns for the two nights differ. Friday night shows a later peak period which coincides with closing of the late-night clubs which provide opportunities for drinking until 2.00 am in the two cities. More generally the peak is between 22.00 hours and 23.00 hours, coinciding with the closing of pubs.

Figures 6.15 and *6.16* show all violent assaults after drinking, plotted on simplified scale maps of the two city centres. The assaults which occurred after 21.00 hours are shown as solid black dots. It was found that most attacks occurred in the principal streets which led directly to late-night public transport facilities. The location of central bus stations, night bus stops and taxi ranks are shown on maps as bold bar lines. The principal routes involved are shown boldly on the map. Of course the data from the study are limited (in Coventry based only on four months), and no doubt stronger patterns would emerge with data drawn from a longer period of time.

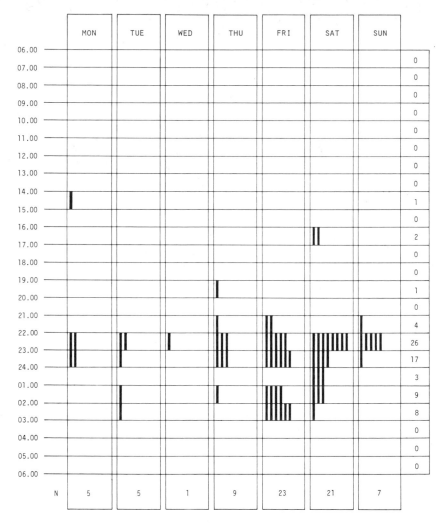

	MON	TUE	WED	THU	FRI	SAT	SUN	
06.00								
07.00								0
08.00								0
09.00								0
10.00								0
11.00								0
12.00								0
13.00								0
14.00								0
15.00								1
16.00								0
17.00								2
18.00								0
19.00								0
20.00								1
21.00								0
22.00								4
23.00								26
24.00								17
01.00								3
02.00								9
03.00								8
04.00								0
05.00								0
06.00								0
N	5	5	1	9	23	21	7	

Figure 6.14 Time chart for fights and brawls after drinking. The chart is based on 58 incidents from a year's data for central Birmingham and 13 incidents from the four months of Coventry data

As these attacks occur at specific times and are confined to a surprisingly limited number of streets, there is a *prima facie* case for policing. British cities at that time of night are much quieter than during the day, particularly in terms of traffic noise. It is possible to hear arguments and disturbances some distance away, and foot patrols are soon aware of disturbances nearby. For the most part the attacks are preceded by shouting and other verbal abuse, and there may be time for some appropriate calming intervention by the police. However, there is also the risk that intervention can lead to assaults on the police.

Of course, there is nothing new in the idea of policing these night routes. The police already give particular attention to the crowds that turn out from pubs and dance-halls, and the police were always about at these times in the two cities studied. It was not the purpose of this study to

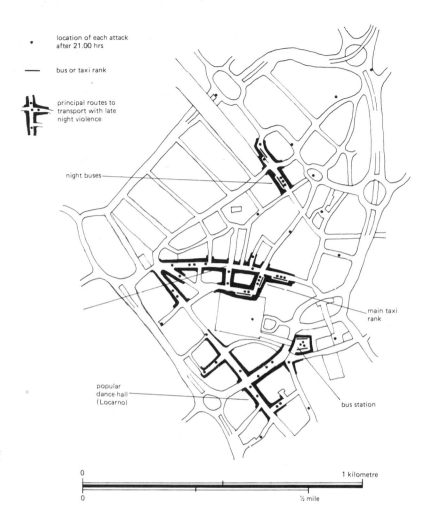

Legend on figure:
- location of each attack after 21.00 hrs
- bus or taxi rank
- principal routes to transport with late night violence

night buses

main taxi rank

popular dance-hall (Locarno)

bus station

0   1 kilometre

0   ½ mile

Figure 6.15 Distribution of fights and brawls after drinking in central Birmingham

assess the effectiveness of present police practice, but with such a precise problem in time and space, there is every opportunity to experiment with different policing techniques. There are obvious methodological difficulties in experimenting. Heavy policing might provoke violence and, at the other extreme, the virtual elimination of policing might significantly reduce the reporting of these attacks. However, it is worth stressing that the risk of displacing this kind of violence elsewhere by policing is small.

These attacks are in no way planned; they occur spontaneously. They only occur because the individuals or groups involved come into contact by chance.

Possible urban planning implications
Although policing seems to be the most appropriate means of managing this crime risk, it must be acknowledged that the exact distribution of the policing problem is determined by planning and licencing decisions taken over a

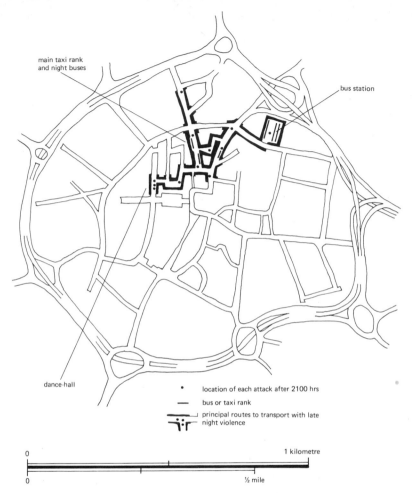

main taxi rank
and night buses

bus station

dance-hall

• location of each attack after 2100 hrs

— bus or taxi rank

principal routes to transport with late
night violence

0   1 kilometre

0   ½ mile

Figure 6.16 Distribution of
fights and brawls after
drinking in central
Coventry

number of years. It may have been fortunate that
the main transport facilities in Coventry were
retained and developed on the same side of the
city as the main places of popular drinking
entertainment. Once a fairly compact pattern is
established, commercial pressures will tend to
reinforce it. For example, all the new developments in the night-life facilities in the centre of
Coventry at the time of the study, such as
late-night take-away food shops and night clubs,
were opening on the central part of the night
route system shown in *Figure 6.16*. It could also

be argued from the shape of the night routes that
the planners' choice of location for the dance-
hall twenty-five years ago was inappropriate as
it would have been better placed nearer the bus
station, which might have almost halved the area
requiring policing.

The Birmingham map in *Figure 6.15* presents
a more complex pattern divided into three sepa-
rate concentrations (dance-hall and bus station;
New Street and the main taxi rank in Stephenson
Street; and Bull Street with the night bus stops).
One reason for the greater complexity is that

80

Birmingham serves a much larger population and there are many more people out on the town drinking. However, it might be argued from the organisation of the map that the location of the night bus stops on the north side of the city centre tends to extend the pattern unnecessarily. It might have been more manageable to have located night bus stops more central to the night life in the city which tends to be in the southern half of the city centre. The pattern which seems to be required in city centres is:

Pattern 6.3
Location of late-night public transport

Late night public transport and the main locations of popular drinking entertainment should be located close together, and preferably in one compact area of a city.

It must be admitted that this pattern is somewhat speculative. It is not known precisely what effect the density of people in the streets has on the probability of this kind of attack occurring. It could be argued that the greater the density the more likely it is that groups and individuals will begin brawling. However, most of these attacks took place in uncrowded conditions without witnesses and so, with more people about, there might be some inhibiting effect.

It is also important to recognise that natural demand and commercial pressures favour this

Figure 6.17 Late-night buses and taxis waiting for the clubs to close in central Coventry shortly before 2.00 a.m. This is at the centre of the night routes shown in Figure 6.16. (Photo by author)

pattern of concentration of popular drinking entertainment around public transport. The more popular pubs in the two city centres tended to be in easy reach of public transport. Also taxi drivers tend to converge on the most popular taxi rank, particularly for the early hours' club trade (see *Figure 6.17*).

Pickpocketing at bus stops
This group of crimes has already been described earlier in this chapter, with details set out graphically in *Figure 6.3*. The crimes involved groups of youths jostling the head of the queue which is boarding a pay-as-you-enter bus at a busy stop in the central shopping district. The youths may have selected their victim, an older man, as he returned his wallet to a back trouser pocket having got out some money to pay his fare. The youths created some diversion while one of them took the wallet from the man's pocket.

As has been pointed out already, this type of crime is both time- and location-specific. The chart in *Figure 6.18* shows that the main time period was Friday from 15.00 to 18.00 hours. This is the time when most wallets would be full, not only from pay-day but also because people would have sufficient money for the weekend.

The description given earlier of the type of bus stop suggests a fairly limited number of locations, and the map in *Figure 6.19* confirms this. Nearly all the bus stops which suffered this pickpocketing were in front of shop windows with a canopy projecting over a wide pavement (see again *Figure 6.4*). All the bus stops shown in *Figure 6.19* are located in the central shopping district. They are only a small proportion of all bus stops which could be located on the map. In practice most of the main streets in the city centre have bus stops every hundred metres or so.

Clearly from both time and location data in *Figure 6.18* and *6.19* there may be a case for policing of the busier of these stops on Friday afternoons. Perhaps more useful would be to

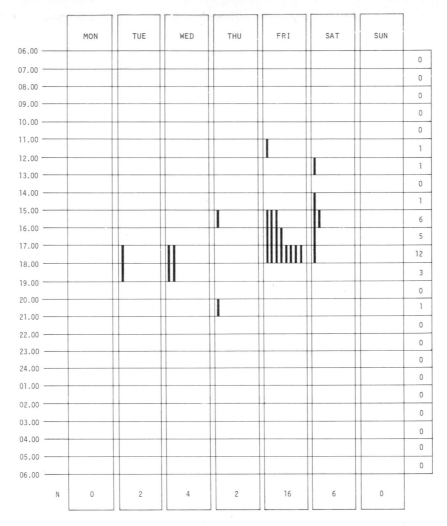

Figure 6.18 Time chart for pickpocketing at bus stops in central Birmingham

alert the transport authority to the problem and hope that bus inspectors who are often on duty in these locations can be on the lookout for likely gangs of youths.

The case for supervision and policing, although theoretically possible, may not be so effective in practice. There are only a limited number of offences in the year, spread over a number of potential locations. At the times when the thefts take place the bus stops are very busy, with some queues having eighty or even one hundred people in them. Each bank of bus stops will have several queues and so it might prove quite uneconomic to police or supervise all the vulnerable bus stops. It may be that environmental measures would be cost-effective because, once installed, they would remain effective with little or no continuing cost.

The environmental measures already suggested were:

Figure 6.19 The locations of pickpocketing at bus stops in central Birmingham

0   1 kilometre

0   ½ mile

- railings or barriers to prevent queue jumping;
- opaque screens or shelter to prevent victim spotting;
- re-siting of stops away from covered shopfronts on wide pavements;
- elimination of pay-as-you-enter buses at rush hours.

The first of these suggestions involves the construction of barriers at the present sites, where cover is available from shop canopies. The use of screens of bus shelters would be more appropriate for stops where there is protection from the weather; this does not apply to the stops where the crime occurs. The re-siting of bus stops away from covered shop-fronts would require some shelter, which coincides with the second suggestion. The fourth solution is probably the most costly, since it requires increased manning of buses or at least some means of selling tickets to queues before buses arrive.

The practical solutions to this crime appear to

83

be either to use some form of barrier at the point of boarding to regulate the queue and prevent potential queue jumping by would-be pickpockets, or to re-site the stops away from covered shop-fronts and provide bus shelters with opaque screens between the queue and any pedestrian area in which youths might loiter. The patterns required might be defined as follows:

Pattern 6.4
Bus stops in busy shopping areas

Bus queues for pay-as-you-enter buses should be either screened from view from passers-by on the same pavement, or marshalled through barriers to prevent queue jumping.

The diagram in *Figure 6.20* illustrates one way in which a marshalling barrier might be arranged.

The use of marshalling barriers at bus stops is not new. Indeed, in the same study, Coventry centre has bus stops in the central shopping area with similar barriers to those shown in the diagram. This is a legacy from the days when the area, which is now for bus traffic only, was heavily trafficked and the barriers were provided to discourage jaywalking. The encouraging fact in the Coventry data was that only one bus stop pickpocketing was reported in the four months' data. It would be wrong to assume that this was solely due to the use of barriers, because there may be many other relevant differences between the two cities; however, the data are very supportive of the theory.

Crime in pedestrian subways
Analysis of the crime groups in the classification in *Table 6.1* showed that in the city centres two types of crime more often occurred in one of the pedestrian subways than elsewhere. They were 'handbag snatches' and 'quick grabs'. Both of these crimes are brief attacks on women. In the case of handbag snatches, the offenders snatched

84

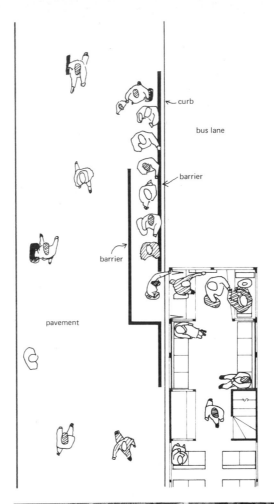

Figure 6.20 A marshalling barrier at a bus boarding point

Figure 6.21 Once into a pedestrian subway system, street traffic and other pedestrian movement are out of sight. A subway in the Birmingham inner ring road. (Photo by author)

the handbag from their victim as they ran past them. The victims' ages ranged widely from the late teens to quite elderly women in their seventies. Some offenders pulled hard, sometimes pulling their victims off-balance, so that they fell to the ground.

The victims of 'quick grabs' were only younger women in the late teens and early twenties. They were alone and walking purposefully, usually on their way to or from work. They were dressed neither casually nor provocatively but probably in a modest smart manner. They were suddenly grabbed, usually from behind, either by the breast(s) or between the legs under the skirt. The victim normally swung around,

screamed or shouted at the offender and pushed him away, or sometimes hit him with a bag. The offender always ran off immediately, sometimes looking back at his victim when well out of reach. In both cases the offenders were youths and younger than their victims. The attacks took place in quiet places, particularly the 'quick grabs'.

Eleven of the eighteen 'quick grabs' found in the city-centre data and eighteen of the thirty-one handbag snatches (all in Birmingham) took place in pedestrian subways or in areas associated with subways (ramps down, etc.). In both types of attack the form of the subways provided 'privacy' for the attack and facilitated escape.

TABLE 6.5 Attacks occurring in or associated with pedestrian subways in Birmingham City Centre

	Number in subways	Number not in subways	% in subways
Fights and brawls after drinking	1	55	2
Attacks made by football supporters	6	12	30
Assaults on children	2	1	67
Other disputes between known persons	1	3	25
Other assaults by strangers	3	19	14
Robbery from a kiosk	1	4	20
Robbery of drunks	4	3	57
Other robbery of people in the street	8	16	33
Handbag snatches	18	13	58
Purses/money snatches from the hand	2	18	10
Other pickpocketing	2	36	5
Thefts from shopping bags	4	201	2
Theft and robbery from children	3	9	27
Unclassified attacks for gain	1	9	10
Quick grabs	6	7	46
Other sexual assaults	1	19	5
Total attacks in subways	63	425	13

Once into one of the subway systems, street traffic and pedestrian movement is out of sight (see *Figure 6.21*). There is little chance of intervention from passing police cars or from passers-by in the street. All offenders were male youths who were no doubt confident of being able to escape by out-running their victims or anyone else who might suddenly appear in the subway.

There were other attacks in the pedestrian subways, particularly in the centre of Birming-ham. Of the total 552 attacks which took place in public spaces in the central area of the city, 63 occurred in pedestrian subways (11%). The full list of the types of attack involved is given in *Table 6.5*. It can be seen from this table that several types of attack seem attracted to the subways in that a high proportion of the robberies occur in subways. Also trouble from football supporters and some crime amongst children seems more likely to occur there.

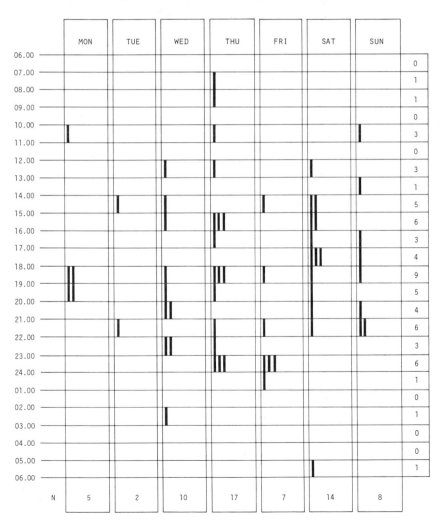

Figure 6.22 Time chart for attacks in pedestrian subways in central Birmingham during 1977–78. Total number of attacks associated with subways in central Birmingham = 63

Figure 6.23 In Coventry the oldest and longest pedestrian subway under the ring road had the most attacks. (Photo by author)

Attacks in pedestrian subways are not specific in time. Unlike the previous three time charts shown for thefts from shopping bags, violence after drinking and bus stop pickpocketing, the time chart for subway crime (*Figure 6.22*) shows no clear pattern. For the most part attacks occur when subways are not busy, even though some of the subways will be very heavily used at other times. This is illustrated to some extent by the appearance of crimes on Sunday, when there would be few people in the city centre. One reason for there being more attacks on Saturday is that this is the day for groups of young football supporters to roam the centre. No explanation has been found for the higher number of attacks on Thursday.

Figure 6.24 An example from another part of the Coventry ring road where, by a different approach to design, the problems of unsafe subways can be eliminated. (Photo by author)

The lack of any clear time pattern excludes policing as a practical crime-prevention measure. It would be quite uneconomic to try to police forty-three subways in the centre of Birmingham throughout the week. The only realistic approach to preventing such crime is through environmental change. The rather limited size of sample available in this study does give some clues about the value of design change in pedestrian subways. There was a tendency in the Birmingham data for most of the subway attacks to occur in the more complex and extensive subway systems, and in Coventry the oldest, longest and narrowest subway had the most attacks (see *Figure 6.23*). In general, the newer parts of the Coventry ring road have junctions which are either elevated above ground level or constructed as underpasses which allow very different designs for pedestrian movement.

The elevated road is the best of all from this point of view. This leaves the ground level with conventional streets and no need for pedestrian subways (see *Figure 6.24*). However, it also seems quite possible to design subways which are far less likely to suffer from crime. None of the Coventry subway attacks occurred in the newer subways which were wide, well-lit, short and opened out onto areas which could be overlooked from nearby traffic lanes and pedestrian areas.

The following patterns for the design of pedestrian routes under roadways seem to be suggested:

Pattern 6.5
Pedestrian subways

Either avoid the need for pedestrian subways under main roads by elevating or lowering road levels to allow pedestrian movement at grade. *Or* where pedestrian subways cannot be avoided they should be as short and wide as possible and open onto spaces which are readily supervised by passing traffic and pedestrians.

7 Protecting schools from crime

Property crime, particularly vandalism, is well established as a problem in schools. The main reasons for this seem to be twofold. Schools are a focus for the activities of young people who are most associated with vandalism, and they are also usually publicly owned institutions, so that the cost of repairs to the buildings can become an issue of political significance. The greatest concern for this problem has been in the United States. A study published by the National Institute of Education in 1977 found that estimates of the annual cost of school vandalism ranged from 50 million to 600 million US dollars. Varying estimates are reported by Zwier and Vaughan (1980) which give the English figure for 1977 as £15 million and New Zealand figures for 1979–80 as about 1.2 million dollars. White (1979) points out that in the United Kingdom nearly half of a local authority's bill for vandalism may be due to damage in schools.

However, these dramatic figures may be a little misleading because of the difficulty over the definition of vandalism. Most of the reporting of damage is through school authorities, particularly building departments, who make little distinction between damage from accidental or malicious activity. A broken window might have been the result of accidental damage from a ball game, or it may have happened as a result of children intentionally throwing stones at windows, or it may even be due to a break-in.

This confusion between accidental and criminal damage occurs in the literature on prevention. For example, a well-illustrated publication by John Zeisel is sub-titled 'Design and administrative guidelines to reduce vandalism' (Zeisel 1976), but it includes examples of damage which cannot be reasonably described as vandalism – i.e. damage to grass areas from short-cut paths across grass and from automobiles parked on grassy areas. Clearly, a school is certain to suffer heavy wear and tear from such a concentration of active young people and must be designed with this in mind. However, this is a different issue from crime prevention.

Even if we confine our definition of vandalism to intentional damage, there seems to be a broader use of the term in the USA than in the UK. Olson and Carpenter (1971) address their study of vandalism to 'Destruction, defacement, thievery, illegal entry and window breakage'. An American study by Pablant and Baxter (discussed later in this chapter) uses data on break-ins to define operationally the difference between high and low levels of vandalism. In this chapter vandalism includes any deliberate damage to school property, whether or not it involves a break-in. The two research studies discussed in detail at the end of the chapter involve break-ins leading to damage or theft or both.

Target hardening

The literature on architectural aspects of vandalism is dominated by the idea of target hardening. Modern school design, particularly in Britain, has created lightweight building systems with very large areas of glass which are much more easily damaged than traditional structures. The breakage of glass is a common problem. Its replacement in frequently damaged areas by stronger materials has been recommended (e.g. Gladstone, 1980), but this may not be so easy to implement owing to the increased cost and operational changes required to introduce the use of toughened glass and polycarbonates (Hope and Murphy, 1983). Other ways of protecting glass would be through design which reduced areas of glass, particularly low-level glass. The most effective form of target hardening is 'target elimination'.

Much of the practice of target hardening has been derived from common sense and experience rather than research and will therefore not be discussed here in detail. However, two valuable references include an architectural checklist of the many kinds of damage which is used by the Consortium for Method Building (see appendix to Sykes, 1979) and John Zeisel's 'Stopping School Property Damage' (Zeisel, 1976) which offers solutions in the US context.

Scope for social measures

One of the assumptions behind this book is that social measures are not likely to be the most effective form of crime prevention. However, there does seem to be some evidence that changes in the social system could be effective in reducing crime within a school. Unlike the residential setting or behaviour in public places the school does have a closely structured social system and a system of authority.

In their survey of American schools, Olson and Carpenter (1971) found that high levels of vandalism occurred in large schools. In contrast, schools which were regarded as 'orderly' and which had 'enthusiastic' student attitudes had relatively low levels of vandalism. Zwier and Vaughan (1980) have compiled an excellent review of literature on school vandalism, much of which deals with social organisation and student attitudes. It is reasonable to believe that methods of teaching, curriculum design and school organisation can be changed or modified and may all have a place in crime prevention.

Recognising the social nature of the problem, Hope (1980) refers to four approaches to preventing property crime in schools – the therapeutic approach, school reform, involvement and opportunity reduction. The weight of his

argument is in favour of opportunity reduction, but perhaps the most significant fact in his argument was that most damage occurs outside school hours. An estimate from Bedfordshire County Council was that 80% of school vandalism took place when the schools were closed. The pattern was supported by other data reported to the Home Office Crime Prevention Centre. If this is the case, it follows that the vandals are not necessarily students or pupils of the school, and any social changes within the school are unlikely to have a major impact on their behaviour. The school, therefore, appears to provide a suitable target for environmental crime prevention measures.

CPTED programme

One of the problems of understanding crime in schools is that there is no methodical record of the various types of criminal behaviour. However, a project in the CPTED programme (see Chapter 1) which dealt with crime prevention in schools (Wallis and Ford, 1980) did produce a

TABLE 7.1 Offences recorded by Broward County Schools System, Florida *(from Wallis and Ford, 1980:14)*

Offences	1973–74	1974–75	% increase
Vandalism	110	183	66.4
Breaking and entering	111	318	186.5
Thefts	499	740	48.3
Assaults	323	484	49.8
Extortion	39	51	30.8
Totals	1082	1776	64.1

rather surprising analysis from the Internal Affairs Department of the Broward County Schools System. The data are set out in *Table 7.1*. They appear to show that the number of reported incidents of vandalism may be less important than breaking and entering, theft and assault. It certainly gives a very different impression of school crime than the British literature, but without much more knowledge of the systems for reporting it is not possible to draw any conclusion.

It is really a great pity that this CPTED School Demonstration Project was a virtual failure, because it appears to be the only really extensive attempt to explore measures of crime prevention in schools which do not involve target hardening. The demonstration involved four high schools which were known to have crime problems. The aim of the project was to reduce fear and crime and so improve the quality of life and the educational experience of the school. This was to be done by providing activities and amenities which it was expected would increase the student identification with the school and particular areas in it. The theory owes a great deal to Newman's ideas (1972) in that it was concerned to enhance territorial identification in the belief that this would lead students to defend the school against intruders or internal disturbances.

'The educational function of schools and the attitude of the Broward County students, faculty, and community were generally opposed to traditional target-hardening mechanisms for crime prevention (e.g. gates, locks and fences). Only in the last resort were such fortress-like mechanisms to be utilised. Rather, the thrust was to be an open, natural environment in which casual surveillance, enhanced activities, and improved motivation would provide the principal deterrents to crime'. (Wallis and Ford, 1980: 17)

One reason that the demonstration project failed was that the evaluation was ineffective. The implementation of measures was slow and incomplete and the collection of data on crime was inconsistent. Even if the project had been well evaluated it would be difficult to know what general principles had been tested. The definitions of CPTED strategies recommended for schools are so poorly designed that it would be difficult for a designer to know what they really mean. For example, under 'classroom

90

problems and strategies' one problem is defined as:
'Location and design definition of multiple-purpose classrooms produces unclear transitional zones, decreases territorial concern, and decreases natural surveillance. Thefts occur.'

The report then lists two strategies for dealing with this problem:
'Extend the identity of surrounding spaces to multiple-purpose space to increase territorial concern and natural surveillance.'

'Provide a functional activity in problem areas to increase territorial concern and natural surveillance'.

What can designers make of such repetitive statements? The definition of the problem is baffling, let alone the fact that it does not explain why thefts should occur. The report contains about thirty CPTED strategies for schools; some are a little clearer in their meaning but generally they lack any prescriptive clarity.

Preventing school break-ins
In contrast to the uncertain findings of the CPTED project, there are two modest research studies on crime in schools which are worth looking at in more detail. They are both based on data about break-ins rather than vandalism. No doubt this provided a more reliable database for research. The first study was carried out in Houston, Texas on a sample of 16 matched pairs of schools, and the second examined 59 school sites in the Inner London Education Authority area. The British study is specific about the subject as it is called *Burglary in Schools: The Prospects for Prevention* (Hope, 1982). The American study may be confused with research on vandalism as it is called 'Environmental Correlates of School Vandalism' (Pablant and Baxter, 1975), '. . . the amount of vandalism . . . was operationally defined as the number of forcible entries with consequent theft or damage'.

The Houston study was designed to explore a large list of environmental variables while attempting to control social factors, such as size of school, ethnic aspects, types of school and neighbourhood income level. For the most part, this matching was achieved by selecting schools which were close together. One of the matched pair would have a high rate of break-ins (HV) and the other a low rate (LV). HV schools had at least twice the number of break-ins as LV schools.

Each of the 29 environmental variables was scored by three judges (observers) on a simple three-point scale during visits to each of the 32 schools. The variables are listed in *Table 7.2* and expressed in the form thought most likely to correlate to break-ins. The mean values for the HV and LV schools are shown separately for comparison, and the difference between these values is measured by a Mann–Whitney U-test. Taking those variables which show significant differences between high and low levels of break-in, three quite clear patterns seem to emerge:

Pattern 7.1
A well-kept school

If school buildings are well maintained, clean, trim, and tidy, and the grounds attractively landscaped with grass mown and paths swept, there appears to be less risk of break-ins.

The pattern is based on items 1, 5 and 7 in *Table 7.2*. These all show significant differences between HV and LV schools. These findings correspond to the general idea that quick repair and maintenance discourages vandalism (Clarke, 1978:72). The theory here is that individuals tend to treat property better if it appears to be cared for by someone. However, the problem with proving this theory is that it may be tautological. Well-kept grounds may be in that condition because they have been less vandalised.

Perhaps the theory of 'occupancy proxy' is more correct. A well-kept school might be perceived by would-be burglars as indicating the presence of a schoolkeeper living on the site. Irvin Waller (1979) has pointed out that 'occupancy proxy' measures are consistently found to reduce residential burglary.

Pattern 7.2
School located near busy areas

If schools are located in busy areas near thoroughfares with commercial buildings (stores, bars, restaurants, service stations) and public buildings, there is less risk of break-ins.

The principal items in the table which contribute to the pattern are items 11, 12, 13 and 14 on *Table 7.2*. These items all imply that having people about on the street and using nearby facilities are valuable in discouraging would-be burglars. The pattern is therefore very much in line with the ideas discussed by the Home Office research team in *Crime in Public View* (Mayhew *et al.*, 1979). It is also interesting to note that the tendency in modern school planning (certainly in Britain) is to locate schools in quiet areas away from traffic for safety and amenity reasons: another example of how planning trends may have contributed to crime risk.

Pattern 7.3
Visibility of school

School buildings should be located close to the street, and the grounds between the school and the street should be clear to give an unobstructed view of the school, both from the street and any nearby houses. (*See Figure 7.1*)

This pattern follows logically from pattern 7.2, in that without visibility the presence of others nearby has no advantage. This pattern is based primarily on items 21, 24 and 25 on *Table 7.2* but it does rely on the presence of residents, so that it is also linked to items 18, 19 and 22.

It is interesting to note from the last few items in *Table 7.2* that the more conventional security

TABLE 7.2 Environmental variables used to compare high- and low-vandalism schools *(adapted from Pablant and Baxter, 1975, Table 4)*

Items	Means HV	Means LV	Significance levels
1 School buildings neglected: peeling paint, dirt, weeds, unmowed grass	2.37	1.62	0.01
2 Plain, dull appearance, no ornament	2.37	1.75	0.05
3 No variety of form or shape in the building design	2.37	1.93	0.02
4 Several separate buildings	2.56	1.93	n.s.
5 Unattractive school grounds	2.56	1.93	0.02
6 Neighbouring property and sidewalks neglected, unkept yards etc	1.87	1.81	n.s.
7 School, less well-kept than neighbourhood	2.31	1.50	0.01
8 School buildings of similar size to surrounding buildings	1.62	1.31	n.s.
9 Not obviously distinguishable as a school	2.00	1.37	0.05
10 School older than surrounding buildings	1.81	1.56	n.s.
11 Few people seen in area around school	1.68	1.18	0.05
12 Lack of diversity of use, e.g. only residences, few commercial or public buildings	2.50	1.87	0.05
13 School grounds surrounded by local residential streets, not busy thoroughfares	2.43	2.15	0.05
14 No parked cars on surrounding streets and no public or commercial buildings visible from school property	2.25	1.43	0.01
15 Playground and open space closed to public	2.62	2.50	n.s.
16 Large block sizes around school	2.25	2.00	n.s.
17 Small area of school ground occupied by buildings	2.50	2.15	n.s.
18 Low-density housing around school	2.50	1.68	0.02
19 Generally surrounded by unused land	2.25	1.50	0.01
20 Building lines of neighbouring property set back from the street	2.37	1.81	0.01
21 School building set back from street	2.56	2.15	0.05
22 All sides of school facing uninhabited land	1.87	1.25	0.02
23 School grounds delimited by streets rather than other buildings	2.43	2.37	n.s.
24 Large areas of school are not visible from the street due to landscaping	1.87	1.31	0.05
25 Residents' view of school heavily impaired	2.50	1.62	0.01
26 Open entrance to grounds, no fences	1.62	1.25	n.s.
27 Windows near ground unprotected	2.69	2.25	n.s.
28 Little night illumination of school	2.69	2.25	n.s.
29 Poor illumination of neighbourhood	2.87	2.37	0.05

Reprinted with permission from Vol.41, No.4, 1975 issue of *Journal of the American Institute of Planners,* copyright 1975 by the American Institute of Planners (now the American Planning Association), 1313 E. 60th St, Chicago, IL 60637.

measures do not distinguish between HV and LV schools. The lack of fences, the lack of protection to windows near the ground and the lack of illumination at night did not significantly lead to more break-ins.

In the study of schools in the Inner London Education Authority area, Hope (1982) explicitly restricts his concern to burglary reported

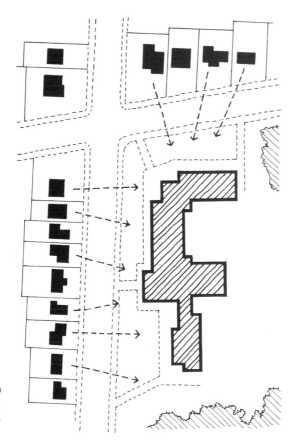

Figure 7.1 School located near main streets with open grounds at the front clearly visible from nearby houses; see pattern 7.3

through school authorities. In selecting a sample of schools he decided to examine secondary schools attended by boys. Inner London Education Authority records showed that secondary schools suffered about three times more burglaries than primary schools. Also, co-educational

and boys-only schools had about twice as many burglaries as girls-only schools. The resulting sample contained 59 different school sites.

From an analysis of records and interviews with school heads and caretakers, Hope concluded that there were three distinct types of burglary in the schools, which were called 'nuisance', 'professional' and 'malicious' burglary. Nuisance burglaries were the most common. Typically, these burglaries may involve local adolescents, maybe some pupils or ex-pupils, who seem to break into the school almost as an end in itself. Usually nothing of much value is stolen unless it happens to have been lying around. Little damage is done. A window may be smashed on entry and internal doors kicked through. Slogans and obscenities may be scrawled on blackboards or walls and a few items of furniture may be broken. Hope sees this kind of delinquency as motivated more by adolescent needs for excitement than a malicious predisposition towards the school.

'Professional' burglaries are the next most common. The purpose of these burglaries seems to be the theft of valuable audio-visual equipment such as video recorders, stereo equipment, and electronic music instruments. These burglaries require more skill in entering the school and breaking into secure stores. 'Malicious' burglary involves intruders damaging certain areas of the school quite severely. Most often damage is done to areas such as the general office or senior teachers' room. Malicious damage may include arson.

In the study, the form of the schools was measured in terms of thirteen variables covering the size and scale of each school and some general characteristics of its layout, design and site planning. It was found that these variables could be combined to form a 'design continuum' of school design. Schools with high scores on the design continuum were large, modern and sprawling. They were likely to have more grassed areas, large areas of glass and varied building height. For convenience Hope labelled this type

TABLE 7.3 Design attributes associated with schools high and low on the design continuum scale *(Hope, 1982:10)*

		Schools low on scale (SOC)	*Schools high on scale (LMS)*
1	Area of buildings	Small	Large
2	Area of site	Small	Large
3	Number of buildings	Few	Many
4	Concentration of buildings	Concentrated	Diffuse
5	Compactness of buildings	Compact	Sprawling
6	Height of tallest building	'Low-rise'	'High-rise'
7	Proportion of single-storey structures	None	Some
8	Amount of glazing	Little	Substantial
9	Age of buildings	Old	Modern
10	Buildings of different ages	Same age	Different ages
11	Density of buildings to site	Dense	Sparse
12	Proportion of site under grass	None	Mostly grass
13	Whether 'landscaped'	None	Trees, flower-beds etc.

of school LMS standing for 'large, modern and sprawling'. Schools with low values on this design continuum were small, old and compact in plan form. Their buildings were on restricted sites devoid of grass, trees and shrubs. They were uniform in height and did not have substantial areas of glazing. These schools were denoted by the letters SOC standing for 'small, old and compact'. The relationship between the thirteen design variables and the design continuum is shown in *Table 7.3*.

The value of this classification of schools into SOC and LMS types is that the design continuum was found to correlate significantly with the incidence of burglary. The nearer that the schools approached the LMS end of the design continuum, there was more likelihood that they would have an increase in burglaries. The smaller, older and more compactly designed schools (SOC) tended to have less burglary. Examples from opposite ends of the design continuum are

94

illustrated in *Figures* 7.2 and 7.3 which are simplified plans of two schools included in the study, drawn to the same scale.

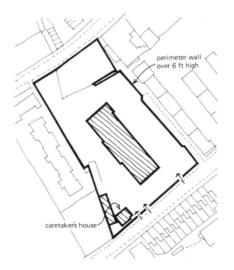

Figure 7.2 Example of a small, old and compact (SOC) school built at the end of the 19th century and surrounded by high walls. It had only one burglary in 1977–8 even though it is in an old and relatively poor multi-racial neighbourhood. Drawn to same scale as Figure 7.3

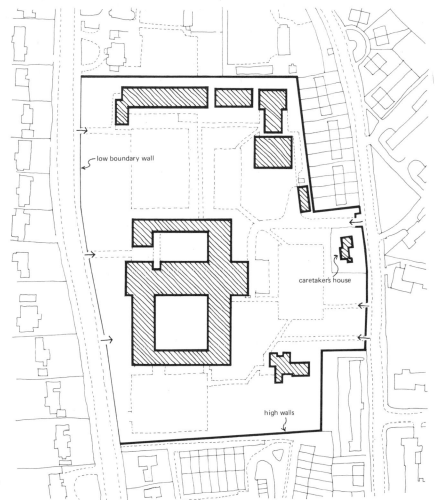

Figure 7.3 Example of a large, modern and sprawling (LMS) school situated in a good, well-established neighbourhood. The boundaries onto adjacent streets were only low walls. There were sixteen burglaries during 1977–8. The plan is to the same scale as Figure 7.2

low boundary wall

caretaker's house

high walls

It is perhaps easy to understand why smallness of scale and compactness of building form are relevant factors in crime prevention, when it is pointed out that caretakers lived in accommodation provided with the school on all sites in the study. Small sites with compact buildings would be much easier to supervise. There may also be other characteristics about the older schools which may have made them more defensible, such as being surrounded by high walls (see

Figure 7.4) and having older-designed windows which were often provided with grilles at lower levels; however, these were not the main focus of the study.

Although there may be many detailed factors which differentiate the SOC and LMS schools, the general finding suggests that to reduce the risk of break-ins at schools where the caretaker lives in, the following pattern is recommended for school design:

Figure 7.4 Example of an SOC (small, old and compact) school in inner London. Typically it is enclosed by high walls and railings and has few entry points which are closed by high gates. The school buildings and grounds are far less accessible and have fewer break-ins than the larger modern post-war school designs which have longer perimeters with several entry points and often only low walls or fencing. (Photo by author)

Pattern 7.4
Scale and compactness of schools

In schools where a resident caretaker lives on the site, the school buildings should be designed to be as compact as possible.

The association of burglary with schools which are large and sprawling is yet another indication of how modern architectural design appears to have contributed to the conditions which give rise to crime.

Although all SOC schools had low burglary rates, LMS schools varied from low to high rates of burglary. It was, therefore, possible to make a comparison between LMS schools with higher and lower rates. One finding was that LMS schools with higher levels of burglary had more accessible roofs. In some ways this might be considered a rather trivial observation but it is a commonly stated requirement that roof access should be limited to reduce vandalism in schools. Zeisel (1976) includes ground-to-roof access as a source of damage to roof-top equipment, skylights, etc. Olson and Carpenter found that many 'natural ladders to roof' correlated positively with high levels of vandalism (1971: table 8). Roof access is also mentioned by Gladstone (1980).

Pattern 7.5
Reduce roof access to schools

All means of climbing onto the roofs of school buildings, particularly single-storey buildings, should be eliminated.

This would include not only the structure of the building, but also climbing plants and trees growing close to the building.

A further finding was that LMS schools with fewer burglaries were more visible at ground level, viewed from the caretaker's house. It would seem logical to extend this to a more precise pattern for the design of schools:

Pattern 7.6
Visibility of school from caretaker's house

There should be a clear view from the caretaker's house of as much of the school as possible, including the most likely approaches to it.

This would not only be an initial design requirement for new schools, but also applies to all future planning of landscaping and extensions to existing schools.

Finally, there was a cluster of findings about the nature of LMS with low burglary rates. They were often more selective in their intake of children, particularly church schools. Although the policy of the ILEA would be to encourage evening use in all schools, these schools tended to hold evening activities which were more school-related (e.g. involving parents) and less to provide for the community in a more general way, such as youth centres.

In this sense these schools probably had more pupil/parent support and were seen less as a public facility. The implications of this seem to be that opening schools to general community use may increase the risk of crime. Clearly the more the school is open to the community the more would-be offenders will have the opportunity to know their way about the school and its grounds, or even have the opportunity to leave windows and doors insecure.

8 Public transport

The public transport systems of most major cities in Europe and North America have suffered an increasing crime problem. Crimes include theft, violence and harassment of passengers, assaults on staff and damage to property. Vandalism is common on railway stations, and buses and trains suffer damage to seats, lighting and other fittings. Perhaps the most dramatic examples of damage to trains have been the wrecking of British trains provided for football supporters and in the United States the famous graffiti that cover the inside and outside of the New York subway trains (Glazer, 1979).

Theft and robbery, now commonly referred to as 'muggings', are reported in large numbers every year on London's Underground. Similarly, staff working on underground stations and buses experience a wide range of abusive behaviour which includes actual violence from passengers. More recently attention has also been given to the problem of violence and harassment of women on the London Underground who have been campaigning for the provision of women-only sections of trains.

Unlike most of the environments discussed in previous chapters, the public-transport environment is supervised through normal operating hours by drivers, conductors, ticket sales and collection staff and other supervisory staff. Buses, trains and transit stations do, therefore, provide a good illustration of how *surveillance by employees* can prevent crime. However, the problems of crime prevention have become more difficult as economic pressures have progressively reduced manning levels in both bus and rail systems. Where at one time buses and trams were normally operated by both a driver and a conductor, they have been replaced in many European cities by one-man-operated buses and trams. Similar changes are taking place on trains and underground railway stations where automatic ticket sales began to reduce manning levels even as early as the 1930s on the London Underground. The use of automatic ticket barriers and simplified fare systems has continued this trend on most urban rail systems.

Protecting the public

There are no comparative figures available for crime on public transport systems in one country, let alone between countries, but it does seem likely that the most common crime problem on underground rail systems is theft from passengers. Certainly, this seems to be the case with the London Underground, which during a peak period in 1974/5 had more than 5000 thefts reported in a year (Burrows, 1980). This figure compared with about 300 assaults on staff (Rose, 1976) and under 100 reported robberies during the same period.

Many of these thefts would be similar to those already described in Chapter 5, such as pickpocketing and purse and bag snatches. From informally visiting stations and talking to staff, it would seem that one common form of 'attack' is similar to the pickpocketing at Birmingham bus stops for pay-as-you-enter buses. A group of youths would jostle potential victims as they were stepping into a train. They would appear to be larking about and making a bit of a disturbance, but were actually creating the opportunity to pick a pocket. The victim would be pushed in the back, his pocket picked and the wallet or purse quickly passed to another member of the group to minimise detection. The victim would probably not realise that his pocket had been picked until he was aboard the train the automatic doors had closed, cutting him off from the thieves who had stepped back onto the platform. By the time the victim could raise the alarm the offenders would have disappeared.

An effort was made on the London Underground to control the problem of theft; and indeed there was a more general concern for the safety of passengers as a whole as a number of more serious attacks had been reported. The part of the system to suffer most was the southern sector. Initially, a special policing effort was launched to deal with the problem on this part of the system, which was followed by the installation of closed-circuit television (CCTV) at four stations (Stockwell, Clapham North, Clapham South and Brixton). Cameras with microphones were mounted to cover platform areas, concourses, areas at the top and bottom of escalators and ticket halls. Most of the cameras could be readily seen by the public and, at least initially, notices were posed to inform the public that a CCTV system was in use.

The introduction of electronic surveillance at the four stations gave Home Office researchers an opportunity to evaluate CCTV as a crime prevention measure. It had been hoped that a comparison could be made between the effectiveness of various policing strategies and the CCTV surveillance, but insufficient information was available about the exact nature of the policing effort to make this possible. However, the figures in *Table 8.1* show that both forms of prevention appear to reduce thefts.

In the four stations in which CCTV was eventually installed, special policing reduced thefts to 60% of what they had been in the previous full year. Some improvement was also found in the rest of the southern sector which had also received additional policing, whereas the level of theft in other parts of the system remained about the same though slightly reduced. When CCTV was installed the number of thefts in the four stations more than halved to 27% of the original figure. However, although this is an impressive reduction, it has to be pointed out that the system as a whole experienced a drop of a third in the number of thefts. The reasons for this are not known, but such an unexplained change must always raise doubts about any conclusions from the evaluation and illustrates well the difficulties that face researchers. Even so the figures in *Table 8.1* suggest that CCTV did reduce the levels of theft in the four stations and must, therefore, have been effective in deterring some of the offenders.

One of the common criticisms of situational crime prevention measures is that they do little

TABLE 8.1 The effects of special policing and CCTV on theft on the London Underground

	12 months before special policing and CCTV	12 months of special policing	First 12 months of CCTV
Stations with CCTV (*n* = 4)	243 (100%)	145 (60%)	66 (27%)
Other southern sector stations (*n* = 15)	535 (100%)	426 (80%)	393 (73%)
Other stations (*n* = 228)	4884 (100%)	4490 (92%)	2962 (61%)

Source: Burrows, 1980 plus private communication.

Note that the 12 months of special policing was calculated from 14 months of data multiplied by 12/14.

more than displace crime elsewhere. The Underground system would provide the easiest means imaginable for displacement as groups of youths could easily take a ride to other stations. Burrows concluded that there probably had been displacement to other stations on the southern sector. To overcome such an objection would mean generally increasing the extent of CCTV which would increase the cost of the programme. Another point to be remembered is that the evaluation was for one year only following installation and this had been preceded by increased police activity. There may have been a reduction of the effect in following years.

All stations involved in this evaluation were deep underground stations with long escalators and a complex of underground pedestrian tunnels and platforms which without some electronic assistance would be imposile to supervise with normal levels of staffing. Several American studies for the design of new subway systems have concluded that more should be done to maximise the surveillance characteristics of stations.

Perhaps the best example is the Washington Metro. Much effort was given to creating a safe environment for the public to encourage them to use the system. Underground stations have been designed spaciously so that passengers can see the whole platform area from any point on the platform. Columns, booths and other obstructions have been minimised to maximise the 'wide-open' concept. Not only has the principle of maximum surveillance been applied to the platform areas but also to the access from the street which has been made as short and direct as possible, quite unlike the deep London stations even on its new extensions. In areas where these principles could not be fully adopted, surveillance is backed up with closed-circuit television, which covers blind spots in entrances, exits and on platforms.

The Washington Metro seems to have been successful in controlling the development of crime common in older subway systems. It has even been claimed that crime had been reduced in the areas where stations had been opened (Crosby, 1978). However, no detailed evaluation is known to the author which can validate the contribution of design measures. It is difficult to know whether a small system is likely to suffer from as much crime as the larger systems such as in New York and London. There were also a number of other measures taken by the Washington Metro which could have explained the success of the new system. For example, there was a good deal of policing in the early stages of its operation, and there is a sophisticated communications system linking trains, station staff and the local police.

It is clear from the evaluation of CCTV on the Underground that surveillance probably does reduce theft, and it seems likely, from the experience of designing a system to reduce the problems of surveillance, that the deliberate improvement of surveillance characteristics and/or systems on underground railways will reduce opportunities for crime. The following pattern would seem to summarise these findings:

Pattern 8.1
Surveillance on underground railway stations

All station areas should be planned so that they can be viewed from either
(a) a permanently staffed observation point, or
(b) a closed-circuit television system.
All staff should have immediate means of summoning assistance from local police or other suitable security personnel.

Although this pattern is known to reduce thefts on station platforms, it seems likely that it would be effective in discouraging other criminal activity such as violent assaults, robbery and vandalism.

Protecting property
It has been shown that surveillance on buses is a deterrent to vandalism. A particularly

TABLE 8.2 Mean seat damage score by deck and type of bus

	One-man-operated (n = 48)	Dual-purpose* (n = 22)	Two-man-operated front entry (n = 12)	Two-man-operated rear entry (n = 17)
Upper deck	5.12	2.47	2.70	1.97
Lower deck	0.22	0.12	0.23	0.37

* Dual-purpose buses were designed for either one- or two-man operation. At the time of the study the Transport Authority estimated these buses to be used as two-man-operated buses for 80% of the time.

well-designed study was made of damage to buses in Manchester (Sturman, 1980), at a time when several types of double-deck buses were in use, including both one-man-operated buses and buses with both driver and conductor. Data on vandalism were collected by careful observation of a sample of ninety-nine buses. Sturman spent many hours at night while the buses were off the road meticulously counting holes, tears, graffiti and scratches around each seat and scoring for the size of each damaged area. Analysis suggested that whereas holes, tears and graffiti were commonly associated together, scratches were not, and so the first three were used as the basis for a measure of vandalism. Scratches were omitted as they seemed more likely to be the result of accidental damage from baskets, umbrellas etc.

Table 8.2 shows the scores averaged for each seat and compared across the four different types of bus and between the upper and lower decks. The first striking pattern in these figures is that the mean damage score for the upper deck is always many times that of the lower deck. This might be partly due to the fact that those who use the lower deck are more often those groups who are less likely to do any damage such as the elderly and mothers with small children. Those groups most likely to cause damage, unaccompanied boys and youths, are most likely to use the upper decks. Another likely reason for this difference is that the bus crews are mostly on the lower deck and able to supervise, which may be why boys and youths prefer the top deck.

The next most clearly marked feature of this data is that the upper decks of the one-man-

TABLE 8.3 Mean damage score for different parts of the upper decks of the four types of bus

	One-man-operated (n = 48)	Dual-operated (n = 22)	Two-man-operated, front entry (n = 12)	Two-man-operated, rear entry (n = 17)
Front	2.55	0.81 ◀	1.30 ◀	1.68
Centre	3.25 ◀	1.27	0.91	1.16
Rear	6.22	2.42	2.83	1.58
Back seat	18.10	11.55	12.96	9.53 ◀

◀ Arrows indicate the position of the staircase.

operated buses are much more heavily damaged than the buses normally operated with a conductor. This seems to indicate quite clearly that even though conductors probably spend most of their time on the lower deck, their presence on the bus significantly reduces the damage to the upper deck. It should perhaps be emphasised that the relatively more serious damage done to the one-man-operated buses had a significant cost implication for the transport authority. Even though the one-man-operated buses were much newer than the other buses in the sample, replacement seats made of hard-wearing plastic had already been fitted on these buses.

In addition to the presence or absence of a conductor on the bus, the amount of vandalism on the top deck appears to have been influenced by the location of the staircase. In *Table 8.3* the mean damage scores are shown for four zones of the upper deck. A common factor to all these distributions is that damage is greatest on the back seat. As we might expect from the more general finding about the presence of a conductor, the highest levels of damage are on the back seat of the one-man-operated buses. There is also a difference between two-man-operated buses depending on whether the staircase is at the front or rear of the bus. The oldest most traditional bus design has the stair at the rear and has the lowest damage to the back seat. This suggests that, providing there is a conductor, the constant risk that the conductor may come up the stairs deters vandals both in the back seat and to some extent the rear of the deck as a whole.

The study is presented here partly because it was an early study in the development of ideas about situational crime prevention, and also because it illustrates the value of supervision by transport staff in preventing vandalism. It also demonstrates the need for designers and operational managers to recognise that changes in the design and operation of buses, as in the case of the one-man-operated buses, can have quite substantial effects on levels of vandalism and

Figure 8.1 A study of damage on buses in Manchester showed that one-man-operated buses had far more vandalism on the upper deck than the older two-man-operated buses. One-man-operated buses in Manchester of similar design to those in the study. (Photo by author)

therefore costs. It is clear that the change over to one-man operation may require much more radical thinking about bus design than just modifying the layout to allow for front entry.

Of course there may be the need to *target harden* the more vulnerable parts of the bus by using more damage-resistant materials, but there may be ways of changing the pattern of movement of passengers through the bus and the use of alternative seat layouts which reduce damage. For example, it might be worth researching the effect of seat layouts at the rear of the upper deck as in *Figure 8.3* which is already in use on the lower deck in some bus designs. Other possibilities might be the use of CCTV as is already in use on some long-distance two-deck coaches in Europe. Again it may be found that

Figure 8.2 The traditional two-man-operated double-decker buses with rear entrances suffered less vandalism than modern one-man-operated buses. At the time of writing London is the only major British city to have large numbers of this type of bus still operating. (Photo by author)

an increased use of single-deck buses may have operational advantages for one-man operation in Britain following the normal practice of most other countries. All these alternatives need good evaluative research. Let us hope that more studies will emerge in due course.

Further evidence that situational measures have been successful in dealing with property damage on public transport comes from two rail examples mentioned at the beginning of the

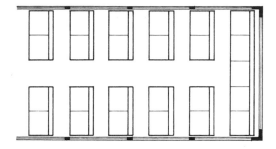

the conventional rear seat layout of front entry buses — those at the back can damage seats unseen by other passengers, also they can damage the back seats in front of them

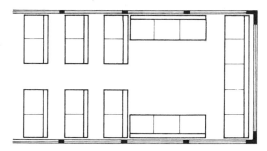

Figure 8.3 Alternative seat layouts for the rear of one-man-operated buses

non-traditional layout with less opportunity for damage to be done to rear seats

chapter. Hooliganism from football supporters on trains in Britain has been greatly reduced, first by not providing special trains for matches where trouble was expected to be serious (target removal), and secondly by selling tickets for special trains only through supporters' clubs who have the responsibility to provide stewards to supervise each carriage (surveillance).

It has been reported that part of the problem of graffiti on the New York subway has been solved by guarding the trains when not in use. Most of the external graffiti were put on the cars while the trains were in the rail yards. By surrounding the yard with a double chain-link fence and using guard dogs, the graffiti have been virtually stopped (*Daily Mail*, 1981). If the report is correct, the defensive measures would seem very cost-effective as the transit authority is said to have spent about $10 million each year removing graffiti.

Protecting employees

Although it is clear that the presence of transport staff can reduce the likelihood of crime, it must also be noted that they too can become the victims. A further consequence of the trend to one-man-operation buses seems to have been an increase in theft or robbery from drivers. Although abuse, assaults and arguments about paying the right fare have always been known with two-man operations (see Rose, 1976), the move to single-manning must seem more potentially threatening to the driver as there is no immediate source of help as there was with two-man operation.

Most experience of this has come from the United States where one-man-operated buses have been common for many years. To combat the growing number of robberies of change and fare money from bus drivers in Washington D.C. a fare system was introduced in which the driver handled no money but would issue a redeemable coupon to passengers who needed change. This led to a dramatic drop in assaults on drivers in the trial period. The system was then permanently introduced. The system has been simplified still further to an exact fare system. Passengers place money in a chute in view of the driver, so that the driver can check that it is the correct fare, but he never handles or has access to any of the money. This is another form of what Clarke and Mayhew (1980) have called *target removal*.

Other forms of protection for drivers have been tried, but evaluations are hard to come by. For example, following the introduction of one-man-operated trams in Götenburg, Sweden, the rise in assaults and other disturbances on trams led to the physical protection of the driver and a ban on the drinking of alcohol in trams and buses (Brodie, 1979). The same source reports that in the Munich public transport system, there is one-man operation on all buses and trains with automatic ticketing and fare sales. The result appears to be a alienation between passengers and the system resulting in increased vandalism and disturbances which led to the use of a special civilian security service.

In Los Angeles, in addition to security patrols, measures adopted for the protection of bus drivers include silent alarms, two-way radios and a system of flashing lights to attract attention if a driver is in difficulty. All these illustrate the range of situational measures that might be considered. All of them were reported as successful. It would be interesting to see what carefully designed research evaluations would actually find!

Some of these principles of protection for staff can be translated into solutions for underground rail and metro systems. In the study by Rose (1976) of violence to staff on London Transport, it appears that staff on the London Underground were a little more likely to be assaulted than bus crews. The risk of assault in 1974/5 on the buses was about thirteen assaults for every hundred staff and on the Underground the risk was nineteen assaults for every hundred staff in a year. The main location of the assaults on the Underground was at the ticket barrier.

One approach to the prevention of these assaults from passengers would be to train and select staff to be able to deal with passengers more skilfully or more tactfully, as Rose suggested in his report (1978). However, the approach adopted in the Washington Metro concentrated on designing the technology of the

Figure 8.4 Automatic ticket barriers at a station on the Washington Metro. The supervisor is located in the kiosk on the right but has no direct contact with the public. All money transactions by the passengers are with machines, some of which are shown on the left of the photograph. (Photo by author)

ticketing such that the staff responsible do not have contact with the public except in an emergency or when the automatic equipment fails (see *Figure 8.4*).

Ticketing at each station is done automatically. Machines issue tickets for whatever value passengers choose, with the information recorded magnetically on the ticket. Each time passengers pass through the system at the entrance or exits, the ticketing barriers record the journey made and deduct the appropriate fare from the ticket until the value of the ticket is insufficient to pay. Passengers can then either calculate with the help of a ticket machine how much is left on the ticket and top it up to complete the journey, or they can have the unused value refunded and buy another new ticket. All money transactions are with machines. The staff do not handle money.

The stations are supervised by an operator in an observation booth placed by the ticketing. Under normal operation the official simply observes the facility and the working and use of the various machines and is therefore out of reach of any assault or abuse from the public. If it is necessary to leave the booth to intervene in some problem, there is always the option of calling help first, either from other staff or if necessary the local police.

All these developments in the use of technology certainly change the risk of crime. What is particularly challenging is how well the changes in job design can be managed. It is quite clear that these changes in technology radically change the nature of the work done by the transport staff and the social system in which they work. It may be that the technology will not be enough, or that some forms of human interaction will have to be reintroduced. We wait to see!

9 Summary of patterns

The thirty-one pattern statements defined through Chapters 3–8 and printed in bold type are set out below for quick reference. They are grouped under several general headings but have the original numbering based on chapter location.

Each pattern was derived from studies of specific crimes or groups of crime. To clarify the purpose of each pattern, the types of crime which the patterns are intended to prevent are indicated by a number code in brackets after the pattern heading. Where a crime type was specifically referred to in research, it is shown in bold type, but where crime was defined less specifically or where it seems reasonable to assume that other crimes may be reduced they are shown in light type. The crime type codes are as follows:

1 vandalism, property damage;
2 burglary, break-ins;
3 robbery (theft with force or threat), snatches;
4 surreptitious theft from the person, e.g. pick-pocketing;
5 violent assault, rowdy behaviour;
6 sexual interference or assault.

Neighbourhood patterns for crime prevention

3.1 Street closure and privatisation (1,2,3)
(a) Access on foot and by car to residential streets or groups of streets, should be limited to avoid through movement: e.g. cul-de-sac or return-loop layout forms.
(b) Any access point should be narrowed and formed as a gateway to symbolise privatisation.
(c) Some form of common management or shared legal responsibility for the street is preferred.

3.2 Homogeneous residential areas (1,2,3)
Residential neighbourhoods should be homogeneously developed as housing and not mixed with other uses, particularly commercial uses and vacant land.

3.3 Single-family housing preferred building form (1,2,3)
Preference should always be given to single-family housing units, and the minimisation of the number of units in any one multi-family structure.

3.4 Limit access to neighbourhoods (1,2,3)
Access to each residential area of say up to 4000 dwellings should be relatively restricted, certainly by road and probably by pedestrian access. Main routes should not pass through neighbourhoods or even provide their boundaries.

3.5 Separation from commercial uses (1,2,3)
Residential areas should be kept separate from commercial uses as far as possible.

4.1 Location of poorer housing (2)
Areas of wealthy or middle-class/middle income housing should be separated as far as possible from poorer housing.

Crime-reducing patterns for housing design

4.5 Houses and through-routes (2)
Houses should not face onto main through-roads, and should preferably not be easily visible from such routes. Houses should face onto and be accessed only from side roads.

4.6 Surveillability of houses (2)

Accessible sides of houses should be relatively open and unobstructed by walls, trees or other landscape and they should be close to the street and to other houses which overlook them.

4.7 Access to rear of house (2)

There should be no open access from the front to the rear of a house. Access might be restricted to full-height locked gates.

4.8 Accessibility of row/terrace houses (2)

(a) The back garden or yard of a terraced house should be surrounded by a 6 ft (1.8 m) high fence or wall unless the windows are guarded.
(b) If the above is not possible at the front of the house it should at least face the street (see pattern 4.6).

4.9 Layout of plots for large detached houses (2)

Plots with large detached houses are best planned adjacent to each other or to inaccessible land and not adjacent to open land.

4.10 Mixed development of houses (2)

In any housing layout or in-fill development, vary the size and room composition of houses to maximise the likelihood of a mixture of occupancies – families with children, retired people, extended families, mixed with households entirely composed of working adults (cf. pattern 5.2).

4.11 Securing windows and doors (2)

Significantly improve the strength and access resistance of all accessible windows and doors uniformly. It would not suffice to simply add locks and similar devices; the use of stronger materials and frames, grilles, etc. should be considered. There is little point in restricting measures to a proportion of access points.

5.1 Preferred access form for dwellings (1,2,3)

Access to dwellings should be as direct as possible from public areas, without intermediate semi-private and semi-public spaces.

5.3 Public areas in housing schemes (1)

Objects and surfaces in public areas of housing schemes (particularly in public housing) should be 'hardened' to reduce risk of damage or removed.

Patterns for multi-unit apartment buildings

4.2 Entrances to apartment buildings (1,2)

The common entrance to an apartment building must be either manned by doormen or similar security personnel, or kept locked with the potential of human surveillance through electronic means. The human element should include resident management or caretaking staff.

4.3 Doors to apartments (2)

The doors to apartments should be strongly constructed with a good locking system. Any surrounding structure should be at least as strong as the door (e.g. avoid use of delivery hatches next to the door or glazed toplights over the entrance doors).

4.4 Arrangement of apartment doors (2)

Doors to apartments should not be isolated from areas used by other residents, but grouped in lobbies serving several apartments. Spy-holes in doors would probably contribute to a potential burglar's perceived risk.

5.2 Allocation and child density (1)

If an apartment building has substantial unsupervised communal areas and lacks any means of access control (pattern 4.2) units should be allocated to as many all-adult households as possible.

Patterns for crime prevention in city centres

6.1 Dispersion of market facilities (4)
Retail market areas in cities should be dispersed to several locations rather than grouped into single large complexes.

6.2 Gangway width in congested markets (4)
Gangways between stalls or counters in congested market areas should be at least 3 m wide.

6.3 Location of late-night public transport (1,3,5)
Late-night public transport and the main locations of popular drinking entertainment should be located close together, and preferably in one compact area of a city.

6.4 Bus stops in busy shopping areas (4)
Bus queues for pay-as-you-enter buses should be either screened from view from passers-by on the same pavement, or marshalled through barriers to prevent queue jumping.

6.5 Pedestrian subways (1,3,5,6)
Either avoid the need for pedestrian subways under main roads by elevating or lowering road levels to allow pedestrian movement at grade. *Or* where pedestrian subways cannot be avoided they should be as short and wide as possible and open onto spaces which are readily supervised by passing traffic and pedestrians.

Patterns for the design and maintenance of schools

7.1 A well-kept school (1,2)
If school buildings are well maintained, clean, trim and tidy, and the grounds attractively landscaped with grass mown and paths swept, there appears to be less risk of break-ins.

7.2 School located near busy areas (1,2)
If schools are located in busy areas near thoroughfares with commercial buildings (stores, bars, restaurants, service stations) and public buildings, there is less risk of break-ins.

7.3 Visibility of school (1,2)
School buildings should be located close to the street, the grounds between the school and the street should be clear to give an unobstructed view of the school, both from the street and from any nearby houses.

7.4 Scale and compactness of schools (1,2)
In a school where a resident caretaker lives on the site, the school buildings should be designed to be as compact as possible.

7.5 Reduce roof access to schools (1,2)
All means of climbing onto the roofs of school buildings, particularly single-storey buildings, should be eliminated.

7.6 Visibility of school from caretaker's house (1,2)
There should be a clear view from the caretaker's house of as much of the school as possible, including the most likely approaches to it.

A pattern for the design of underground railway stations

8.1 Surveillance on underground railway stations (1,3,4,5,6)
All station areas should be planned so that they can be viewed from either
(a) a permanently staffed observation point, or
(b) a closed-circuit television system.
All staff should have immediate means of summoning assistance from local police or other suitable security personnel.

Bibliography

Alexander, C., 1966 'A city is not a tree', *Design,* February, 46–55.

Alexander, C., Ishikawa, S. and Silverstein, A., 1977, *A Pattern Language,* New York, OUP.

Ardrey, R., 1966, *The Territorial Imperative,* New York, Atheneum.

Baldwin, J. and Bottoms, A. E., 1976, *The Urban Criminal,* London, Tavistock Publications.

Bottoms, A. E., '1974 Review of defensible space', *British Journal of Criminology, 14,* 203–206.

Brantingham, P. J. and P. L., 1975, 'The spatial patterning of burglary', *The Harvard Journal, 14,* 2, 11–23

Brantingham, P. J. and P. L., 1981, 'Notes on the geometry of crime', in Brantingham, P. J. and P. L., *Environmental Criminology,* Beverlly Hills, Sage.

Brill, W. H., 1973, 'Security in public housing: a synergistic approach', in *Deterrence of Crime In and Around Residences,* Criminal Justice Monograph, Washington D.C., GPO.

Brodie, M., 1979, *Vandalism and Violence on Public Transport Systems,* Bibliography No. 107, London, Greater London Council.

Brody, S. R., 1976, *The Effectiveness of Sentencing,* Home Office Research Study No. 35, London, HMSO.

Burrows, J., 1980, 'Closed circuit television and crime on the London Underground', in Clarke, R. V. G. and Mayhew, P. (editors), *Designing Out Crime,* London, HMSO.

Cirel, P., Evans, P., McGillis, D. and Whitcomb, D., 1977, *An Exemplary Project: Community Crime Prevention Program. Seattle, Washington,* Washington D.C., GPO.

Clarke, R. V. G. (editor), 1978, *Tackling Vandalism,* Home Office Research Study No. 47, London, HMSO.

Clarke, R. V. G., 1980, 'Situational crime prevention: Theory and Practice', *British Journal of Criminology 20,* 2, April, 136–147.

Clarke, R. V. G. and Mayhew, P. (editors), 1980, *Designing Out Crime,* London, HMSO.

Crosby, T., 1978, 'Crime in D.C.', *Mass Transit 5,* 3 March, 18–19.

Daily Mail, 1981, 'Writing's off the wall', 3 December.

Davidson, R. N., 1981, *Crime and Environment,* London, Croom Helm.

Department of Housing and Urban Development, 1980, *Interagency Urban Initiatives Anti-Crime Program,* First Report to Congress, Washington D.C., GPO.

Department of the Environment, 1971, *Wilful Damage on Housing Estates,* Building Research Station Digest No. 132, London, HMSO.

Fowler, F. J., McCalla, M. E. and Mangione, T. W., 1979, *Reducing Residential Crime and Fear: The Hartford Neighborhood Crime Prevention Program,* Washington D.C., GPO.

Fowler, F. J. and Mangione, T. W., 1982, *Neighborhood Crime, Fear and Social Control: A Second Look at the Hartford Program,* Washington D.C., GPO.

Gardiner, R. A., 1978, *Design for Safe Neighborhoods*, Washington D.C., GPO.

Gladstone, F. J., 1978, 'Vandalism amongst adolescent schoolboys', in Clarke, R. V. G. (editor), *Tackling Vandalism*, Home Office Research Study No. 47, London, HMSO.

Gladstone, F. J., 1980, *Co-ordinating Crime Prevention Efforts*, Home Office Research Study No. 62, London, HMSO.

Glazer, N., 1979, 'The subway graffiti of New York', *New Society*, 11 January, 72–74.

Gould, L. C., 1969, 'The changing structure of property crime in an affluent society', *Social Forces 48*, 50–59.

Greenberg, S. W., Rohe, W. M. and Williams, J. R., 1981, *Safe and Secure Neighborhoods: Physical Characteristics and Informal Territorial Control in High and Low Crime Neighborhoods*, North Carolina, Research Triangle Institute.

Heal, K., 1982, 'The police, research and crime control', *Home Office Research Bulletin, 13*, 16–19.

Hedges, A., Blaber, A. and Mostyn, B., 1980, *Community Planning Project: Cunningham Road Improvement Scheme*, Final Report, London, Social and Community Planning Research.

Herbert, D., 1977, 'Crime, delinquency and the urban environment', *Progress in Human Geography, 1*, 208–239.

Hillier, B., 1973, 'In defence of space', *RIBA Journal*, November, 539–544.

Hollander, B., Hartmann, F. X., Brown, R. R. and Wiles, R., 1980, *Reducing Residential Crime and Fear: The Hartford Neighborhood Crime Prevention Program*, Executive Summary, Washington D.C., GPO.

Home Office, 1981, *Criminal Statistics England and Wales 1980*, London, HMSO.

Hope, T. J., 1980, 'Four approaches to the prevention of property crime in schools', *Oxford Review of Education, 6, 3*.

Hope, T. J., 1982, *Burglary in Schools: The Prospects for Prevention*, Research and Planning Unit Paper 11, London, Home Office.

Hope, T. J. and Murphy, D. J. I., 1983, 'Problems of implementing crime prevention: The experience of a demonstration project', *Howard Journal of Penology and Crime Prevention*. (in press).

Hunter, J., 1978, 'Defensible space in practice', *The Architects' Journal*, 11 October, 675–677.

Jackson, H. and Winchester, S., 1982, 'Which houses are burgled and why', *Home Office Research Bulletin, 13*, 20–21.

Jacobs, J., 1962, *The Death and Life of Great American Cities*, London, Jonathan Cape (also 1964 by Penguin).

Leather, A. and Matthews, A., 1973, 'What the architect can do: A series of design studies', in Ward, C. (editor), *Vandalism*, London, The Architectural Press.

Maguire, M., 1982, *Burglary in a Dwelling: The Offence, the Offender and the Victim*, London, Heinemann.

Mayhew, P., 1979, 'Defensible space: The current status of a crime prevention theory', *The Howard Journal, 18*, 150–159.

Mayhew, P., Clarke, R. V. G., Burrows, J. N., Hough, J. M. and Winchester, S. W. C., 1979, *Crime in Public View*, Home Office Research Study No. 49, London, HMSO.

Musheno, M. C., Levine, J. P. and Palumbo, D. J., 1978, 'Television surveillance and crime prevention: Evaluating an attempt to create defensible space in public housing', *Social Science Quarterly*.

National Institute of Education, 1977, *Violent Schools – Safe Schools: The Safe School Study Report to the Congress, 1,* Washington D.C., GPO.

Newman, O., 1972, *Defensible Space: People and design in the violent city,* New York, Macmillan. (1973. London, The Architectural Press).

Newman, O., 1973, *Architectural Design for Crime Prevention,* National Institution of Law Enforcement and Criminal Justice, Washington D.C., GPO.

Newman, O., 1975, Community of Interest – design for community control, in: *Architecture, Planning and Urban Crime,* Conference proceedings arranged by NACRO, Chichester, Barry Rose.

Newman, O., 1976, *Design Guidelines for Creating Defensible Space,* National Institute of Law Enforcement and Criminal Justice, Washington D.C., GPO.

Newman, O., 1980, *Community of Interest,* New York, Anchor Press/Doubleday.

Newman, O. and Franck, K., 1980, *Factors Influencing Crime and Instability in Urban Housing Developments,* Washington D.C., GPO.

Olson, H. C. and Carpenter, J. B., 1971, *A Survey of Techniques to Reduce Vandalism in Schools,* Mclean, Virginia, USA, Research Analysis Corporation.

Pablant, P. and Baxter, J. C., 1975, 'Environmental correlates of school vandalism', *Journal of American Institute of Planners, 41,* 4, 270–279.

Poyner, B., 1980, *Street Attacks and their Environmental Settings,* The Tavistock Institute of Human Relations (unpublished).

Ramsay, M., 1982, *City-centre crime: The Scope for Situational Prevention,* Research and Planning Unit Paper 10, London, Home Office.

Rees, N., 1981, *Graffiti 3,* London, Unwin Paperbacks.

Reppetto, T. A., 1974, *Residential Crime,* Cambridge, Mass., Ballinger.

Riley, D., 1980, 'An evaluation of a campaign to reduce car thefts', in Clarke, R. V. G. and Mayhew, P., *Designing Out Crime,* London, HMSO.

Riley, D. and Mayhew, P., 1980, *Crime Prevention Policy: An assessment,* Home Office Research Study No. 63, London, HMSO.

Rose, J. S., 1976, *A study of Violence on London Transport,* Behavioural Science Unit, London, Greater London Council.

Rubenstein, H., Murray, C., Motoyama, T., Rouse, W. V. and Titus, R. M., 1980, *The Link Between Crime and the Built Environment: The Current State of Knowledge, 1,* National Institute of Justice, Washington D.C., GPO.

Scarr, H. A., 1973, *Patterns of Burglary,* US Department of Justice, Washington D.C., GPO.

Smith, M., 1980, 'A television-linked entry-phone system to safeguard high-rise tenancies', *Housing, 16,* 3, 10–12.

Smith, M. E. H., 1982, 'TV-linked entry-phone system offers a life-line to high-rise estates', *Housing, 18,* 3, 13–15.

Sturman, A., 1978, 'Measuring vandalism in a city suburb', in Clarke, R. V. G. (editor), *Tackling Vandalism,* Home Office Research Study No. 47, London, HMSO.

Sturman, A., 1980, 'Damage on buses: The effects of supervision', in Clarke, R. V. G. and Mayhew, P. (editors), *Designing Out Crime,* London, HMSO.

Sykes, J. (editor), 1979, *Designing Against Vandalism,* London, Design Council.

Tien, J. M., O'Donnell, V. F., Barnett, A. and Mirchandani, P. B., 1979, *Street Lighting Projects,* National Institute of Law Enforcement and Criminal Justice, Washington, D.C., GPO.

Tighe, C., 1981, 'Blight is banished', *Building Design*, September 16–19.

Waller, I. and Okihiro, N., 1978, *Burglary: The Victim and the Public*, Toronto, University of Toronto Press.

Waller, I., 1979, *What Reduces Residential Burglary: Action and Research in Seattle and Toronto*, Paper presented at Third International Symposium on Victimology, Münster, West Germany.

Wallis, A. and Ford, D., 1980, *Crime Prevention through Environmental Design: An Operational Handbook*, National Institute of Justice, Washington D.C., GPO.

Wallis, A. and Ford, D., 1980, *Crime Prevention Through Environmental Design: The School Demonstration in Broward County, Florida*, Executive Summary, National Institute of Justice, Washington D.C., GPO.

Walsh, D. P., 1978, *Shop-lifting: Controlling a Major Crime*, London, Macmillan.

White, D., 1979, 'Vandalism and theft in schools: How local authorities can defend themselves', in Sykes, J. (editor), *Designing Against Vandalism*, London, Design Council.

Wilson, J. Q., 1975, *Thinking About Crime*, New York, Basic Books.

Wilson, S., 1978, 'Vandalism and defensible space on London housing estates', in Clarke, R. V. G. (editor), *Tackling Vandalism*, Home Office Research Study No. 47, London, HMSO.

Wilson, S., 1981, 'A new look at Newman', *RIBA Journal*, May 50–51.

Winchester, S. and Jackson, H., 1982, *Residential Burglary: The Limits of Prevention*, Home Office Research Study No. 74, London, HMSO.

Zeisel, J., 1976, *Stopping School Property Damage: Design and Administrative Guidelines to Reduce School Vandalism*, Arlington Virginia, American Association of School Administrators.

Zwier, G. and Vaughan, G. M., 1980, *School Vandalism: A Review of Overseas Research*, Wellington, NZ, Department of Education.

Index